THE SALES UPGRADE

MASTERING THE SEVEN Rs OF SELLING

HANS J. VAN ORDER

THE SALES UPGRADE

If you are a talented and ethically grounded sales professional, the most effective way for your customers to get what they want is to do what you tell them to do. Stop "asking for the sale," and start recommending it.

The Sales Upgrade will immerse you in an experiential sales methodology which will allow you to connect on a human level, create value outside of your products and services, and master the many facets of consultative selling.

Based on the patterns and behaviors of the best performing professionals, Hans Van Order has modeled, packaged, and explained a highly successful strategy that can be implemented immediately in any sales environment.

In addition to *The Seven Rs of Selling*, you will learn to STEP Forward, PREACH Luxury, READ Your Customer, LIVE Your Product, and NAVIGATE Price.

Upgrade your profession, upgrade your performance, upgrade your customer's experience, and upgrade your paycheck. Read and apply *The Sales Upgrade*.

Copyright © 2019 by Hans J. Van Order

All rights reserved.

No part of this book may be transmitted or reproduced in any form or by any electronic or mechanical means, including photocopying, recording, or by any information storage and retrieval systems, without prior written, dated permission from the author, except for the use of brief quotations in a book review.

Published in Charlotte, North Carolina by Performance Publishing.

Performance Publishing books may be purchased in bulk (25 or more) for educational, business, fundraising, or sales promotional use. For information, please email books@driveperformance.com

Any questions about the book, rights licensing, or to contact the author, please email: hans@driveperformance.com.

ISBN: 978-1-951903-00-8	Hardcover
ISBN: 978-1-951903-01-5	Paperback
ISBN: 978-1-951903-02-2	Audiobook
ISBN: 978-1-951903-03-9	Kindle edition
ISBN: 978-1-951903-04-6	eBook edition

Book Cover Design: Jason Anscomb

Interior Book Design: Andy Meaden

PRAISE FOR *THE SALES UPGRADE*

"Whether you sell a product, service or concept, *The Sales Upgrade* provides you with the tools to be the best in your field. There are two striking themes running throughout the book: "the idea that selling is about helping," and that regardless of your product segment, you can make each customer interaction "a luxury buying experience." I wish that Hans would have written this book sooner as I've spent the last 30 years in trial and error trying to achieve what he has comprehensively assembled here."
Mark Derengowski, Director Retail Development, Porsche Cars North America

"*The Sales Upgrade* has completely changed my perspective of what selling is all about. This book is an amazing source of tools that will allow us to develop the skills we all need to transform the sales process from the typical feature-benefit product dump into a consultation. This allows both sides to get what they really want, while building a trusting relationship that is rewarding and fulfilling. *The Sales Upgrade* will be a must read for everyone in sales in our distribution channel."
Alejandro Leal, Director General, Importaciones Electrodomésticas S.A., Monterrey, MX

"This is a must read for anyone responsible for sales or sales management. *The Sales Upgrade* is a quick and comprehensive guide on the evolution of retail transformation. The new emphasis on "always caring" vs "always closing" is an extremely important concept for the future. The digitalization of commerce is definitely the game changer that must be embraced in order to be successful."
Rory Anne Hepner, General Manager Strategic Retail Development, Mercedes-Benz USA

"Through his years of speaking to sales audiences, Hans has captured the essence of what it takes to be successful. This book is a necessary read for every sales associate and sales organization as it helps shift salespeople to a more modern selling process. Digitization is here, and modernizing the sales process will ensure relevance for companies as we move into a more consultative sales environment. This book is for every sales person, sales manager, and general manager, even executives not active in the sales process. Thanks for taking the time to make what is seemingly a very difficult transition appear to be a natural and easy process."
Gabriel Haim, Vice President, Sales, Roadster

"The Sales Upgrade *is an excellent addition to the tools of salespeople, sales managers and anyone who desires a structured process for engaging with clients and customers. Hans Van Order collects his three decades' of experience into a highly approachable process for reframing the way sales are initiated, nurtured and closed, resulting in rewarding and profitable relationships. I highly recommend this book to individuals of all experience levels who value the art and science of selling and wish to refine and improve their skills."*

Esther Poulsen, CEO, Raare Solutions

"I recently completed Hans Van Order's latest book: The Sales Upgrade *and enjoyed it immensely. Hans' methodical approach distills decades of sales 'philosophy' and experience into actionable and easy to remember strategies: R7, STEP Forward, PREACH Luxury, READ Your Customer and NAVIGATE Price. An essential tool for the new associate or the life-long sales professional, The Sales Upgrade guides with knowledge, skill and most importantly: responsibility and compassion."*

William Gatti, President & CEO: Trek Development Group

"The Sales Upgrade *is not for the faint of heart – but for those who have heart – which is at the core of this book. It challenges you to be prepared to work; not only to become a better sales professional, but to become a better human, while moving forward in our modern world of technology. Hans' has put his extensive experience in the business of selling to great use as he takes away the perceived "secret formula" of selling and leaves the reader with a solid playbook that can be applied to all phases of life. My "Recommendation" is to read the book, and take it seriously!"*

Gail Fernandez, Manager, Learning and Quality, Mercedes-Benz USA

"Our entire world revolves around the art of consulting luxury clientele, while carefully navigating through the sales process. A fantastic addition to the workshops and seminars we've attended with Hans and his team at Drive Performance; this book serves as both a wake up call and an essential reference for our sales force and inside sales team. The Seven Rs of Selling will guide my team and help bring us to an entirely new level. All while elevating the customer experience. The takeaways will benefit them both on a personal and professional level."

Philippe Hazan, Vice President, Sales and Marketing – Maroline, Inc. Montreal QC

"The Seven Rs of Selling, *delivered in a customized way, provides the rapport and relationship building that produces the 5 star experience every buyer wants and deserves. This book challenges experienced sales professionals to step outside their comfort zone and enjoy greater growth.* The Sales Upgrade *also provides an outstanding template for professionals new to the exciting career of selling."*
Rick Speicher, VP of Operations, Bobby Rahal Automotive Group

"The Sales Upgrade, *is an important contribution to understanding and excelling in the sales process. While "Relationship Selling" has been around for a good number of years with advances over more purely transactional approaches, Hans Van Order pushes this to a new level by reframing the salesperson's role more fully on the consulting end of the spectrum. Having thought long and hard about the nature of sales from his experience, observations and study of human psychology, Van Order sees sales as essentially a helping partnership in discovery and solution development between buyer and seller. His language is crisp and the frameworks presented pragmatic, rich in lively examples. The book itself models the way of one of its key messages: Take the time to see the complexity at hand, then help the client-customer navigate to that which they truly value through successive rounds of clarification. A very worthy read."*
Martin D. Goldberg, Management Consultant & Principal, Distant Drummer LLC

"*Everyone is focused on "Digital Retail," instead of focusing on the reality that it's just "retail." This book helps frame the modern retail consumer experience and ways that a sales person can adapt and adjust to be more customer focused, because the customer is already experiencing modern retail in every other transaction in their life. Helping an automotive salesperson understand the techniques and concepts in* The Sales Upgrade *will better fulfill the customer's needs; both online and in store. In a modern retail environment, this is critical to a better customer experience. Love the book!! It's fundamentally easy to read and has actions that anyone can implement quickly."*
Glenn S. Rizzo, Director Sales Operations, Southeast Toyota Distributors, LLC

CONTENTS

INTRODUCTION	XI
PART ONE: MODERN SALES CONCEPTS	**1**
CHAPTER ONE – REFRAMING THE CONCEPT OF SALES	3
CHAPTER TWO – SELLING IN A DIGITAL WORLD	15
CHAPTER THREE – SALES RESPONSIBILITIES	27
PART TWO: THE CONSULTATIVE SALES FRAMEWORK	**37**
CHAPTER FOUR – THE SEVEN Rs OF SELLING (R7)	39
CHAPTER FIVE – STEP FORWARD	75
CHAPTER SIX – PREACH LUXURY	89
CHAPTER SEVEN – READ YOUR CUSTOMER	115
CHAPTER EIGHT – LIVE YOUR PRODUCT	125
CHAPTER NINE – NAVIGATE PRICE	133
PART THREE: R7 STRATEGIES, EXPANDED	**145**
CHAPTER TEN – R1: RESEARCH REVISITED	147
CHAPTER ELEVEN – R2: INTENTIONAL RAPPORT	165
CHAPTER TWELVE – R3-R4-R5: RECOMMENDATION STATEMENTS	177
CHAPTER THIRTEEN – R6: THE VALUE OF RELATIONSHIPS	189

CHAPTER FOURTEEN – R7: FOCUSING ON RESULTS	199
PART FOUR: TAKING ACTION AND MOVING FORWARD	**209**
CHAPTER FIFTEEN – APPLYING R7	211
CHAPTER SIXTEEN – CUSTOMIZING YOUR SALES UPGRADE	227
CHAPTER SEVENTEEN – FINAL THOUGHTS	243
THANK YOU	**244**
WHAT'S NEXT?	**246**
ACKNOWLEDGEMENTS	**247**
ABOUT THE AUTHOR	**248**

WHO SHOULD READ *THE SALES UPGRADE?*

Sales requires confidence, and a successful career in sales often creates large egos. Great salespeople know that it takes raw talent, a lot of practice, and a willingness to continue to learn and adapt to be successful over the long term. When I am speaking at a sales conference, to break through some of those egos I ask, "Show of hands, on a scale of one to 10, how many of you believe you are a 10 when it comes to sales?" I ask them to keep their hands up and I say, "Keep your hands up if you believe you've peaked. In other words, please keep your hands up if you believe you will never be any better in sales than you are today." At this point, most of the hands go down, and any hands remaining are extremely revealing.

The sales profession is going through an inevitable evolution and it is time to adapt. This book is for anyone who believes their sales performance can improve from where it stands today. If you are "peaking," put this book down. It's not for you. There is no book for you.

Whether you are contemplating a career in sales, just beginning a career in sales, or you are a successful sales "veteran," the framework laid out in this book will help you refine your approach and develop repeatable skills, techniques, tactics, and strategies that will help you improve your performance.

For some of you, this book will put names to the things you are instinctively doing and allow you to mentally frame your own approach. For others, it will completely revolutionize the way you look at the role of a salesperson and provide a proven framework to move forward. During and after many coaching sessions over the years, many individuals have verbalized some version of "Where were you when I started in sales? I could have been using this for years." It was with these individuals in mind that I decided to write *The Sales Upgrade*.

INTRODUCTION

Transactional selling is dying and the in-the-moment experience between the customer and the sales professional has never been more important. The squeezing of margins is inevitable and the price difference between competitors is constantly shrinking. In a world of increasing commoditization and price transparency, the differentiating factors and competitive advantages of products and services have become largely experiential. Consumer behavior is changing and the demand for transparency is increasing. Customer interactions during the sales and purchase process are increasingly digital and the pace of this transformation is accelerating. It's time for an upgrade.

The Sales Upgrade was written to influence a shift in the world of sales for both customers and sales professionals. I believe that the insight and methods laid out in the following pages will revolutionize the way salespeople view themselves and their careers. Consumer preferences are pushing sales teams everywhere to adapt and evolve. The strategies and techniques you will learn in this book are at the very forefront of a movement to transform the way products and services are sold, and eventually change the way consumers view the profession of sales.

Product information, specifications, comparisons, and reviews are readily available at the click of a button. And many of our customers do quite a bit of research before they contact us. As a result, the sales professional's value as a knowledgeable provider of information is diminishing. Our customers often know more than we do about their specific product of interest.

Today's consumers have very little desire, and are much less willing, to enter a traditional "sales situation." In the age of, "Buy now with one click," many potential customers are simply choosing to avoid human contact altogether during the sales process. This trend will continue to increase for most of us unless the sales experience itself can be valuable and positive for the client. Consumers have wanted this change for a long time, and today's alternatives to traditional methods are empowering them to demand it.

The Seven Rs of Selling (R7) encapsulates a "sales belief system." Developed over many years, multiple industries and thousands of scenarios, R7 is a practiced, proven, ethical and successful sales strategy. This strategy may be employed by absolutely anyone wishing to consult, guide, advise, or otherwise influence the decisions, actions or behaviors of another while providing an exceptional experience. In my capacity as a consultant, coach and facilitator, I have helped thousands of individuals apply this strategy to their unique sales situations in many different countries, industries, and environments.

R7 began many years ago through the development of very specific strategies and tactics. As I adapted my materials and resources to new environments, I carried forward the essential methods and approaches that proved worthwhile. Each time I moved from one sales situation to the next, I grew in my understanding of what I considered to be the core sales elements that transcended environment, industry, and situation. I fine-tuned and expanded this core set of skills and behaviors until I instinctively knew that I had created the model for a universal sales methodology.

Over the years, these strategies have adapted, grown, and evolved into The Seven Rs of Selling. The concepts in this book will provide a simple framework to move through the sales process more successfully. This framework is easily understood, easily remembered and easily adapted to any sales situation.

The Sales Upgrade is a passionate sharing and "grand unveiling" of the *The Seven Rs of Selling*. My goal is to help you learn and then apply this strategy to your unique set of circumstances. I will discuss the concepts of sales and "selling" as well as the power of your approach, language, and dialogue in any customer interaction. I will provide you with an overview of the R7 Methodology so you will have a contextual understanding as I dive deeper into some of the universal truths of persuasion and influence. Together, we will explore the affect that a client's experience has on their perception of value as well as their decision-making process. We will break down the sales process and understand the importance of intermediate goals and desired outcomes - not simply this month's performance goals, but the goals of each and every customer touch point.

Questions are the most powerful and versatile tools for anyone engaged in a consultative capacity. I will show you that asking questions can be elevated to an art form. Finally, I will explain the different modes of consultative sales in relation to R7 and walk you through the building blocks of crafting your own unique strategy.

Throughout this book, I will provide specific examples and share many other practices. For the greater part of 30 years I have been deeply involved in improving sales performance, both my own and that of others. In that time, I've been lucky enough to work with, and learn from, some of the very best. I've seen some of the most impactful and successful ways of approaching sales situations. Here, I have simplified, refined and honed these ideas into an extremely powerful framework that is simple to understand and apply. In addition to The Seven Rs of Selling, you will learn to STEP forward, PREACH luxury, READ your customer, LIVE your product and NAVIGATE price. I'm excited to share this with you and I'm confident you will find the journey rewarding.

Many of the ideas shared within these pages will enhance your sales career. However, every sales situation is unique. You bring your own style, talents and understanding to each sale. As you read *The Sales Upgrade*, you will decide which ideas to adopt "right off the shelf," and which to modify and adapt to your environment.

How to Read and Apply The Sales Upgrade:

This book is the accumulation and organization of a lifetime of my own experience, as well as the successful practices and behaviors of thousands of high performing sales professionals. I do not expect you to read, absorb, and put this material into practice in one fell swoop. No one particular model I present is over-elaborate. However, as you begin to see how they intertwine and work together, they can become quite complex.

In order to see the interplay between all of the components, I'd suggest first reading this book once from start to finish. In this way, you will have an understanding of the big picture and a level of confidence with the material. I structured the book to help you build upon each concept as you go. *The Sales Upgrade* should serve as a reference and reminder as you incorporate the concepts into your sales practice, and you return to specific concepts as necessary.

I've organized the book into four parts. In Part One, I introduce sales as a consultative process; discuss the impact of technology and "digital retail" on traditional sales structures; and provide an overview of the many responsibilities of salespeople. I also explain the ethical ramifications of being a persuasive individual in a position of power.

In Part Two, I provide a detailed introduction into the entire consultative framework. This begins with *The Seven Rs of Selling* (R7) and continues with the supporting models. I isolate each model to provide a better individual understanding of each concept. Your head might be swimming with new information at this point. That's perfectly ok.

In Part Three, I dive deeper into R7, with a focus on practical use in combination with the other models introduced in Part Two. I walk through The Seven Rs of Selling with practical examples and I begin combining the different models and concepts you learned in Part Two.

In Part Four, I focus on using R7 in your workplace. I provide advice on how to use these concepts in outbound initiatives, email, and phone communication. I also walk you through some exercises you can do to develop the resources you will need to successfully implement *The Sales Upgrade* in your environment.

Enjoy the read!

PART ONE:

MODERN SALES CONCEPTS

CHAPTER ONE
REFRAMING THE CONCEPT OF SALES

"Authentic selling, in all but the simplest of situations, is a consultative process."

WHAT DOES IT MEAN TO SELL?

During speaking engagements, I often ask my audience questions like, "What is sales? What does it mean to sell? What precisely are we doing when we are selling?" I hear answers anywhere from, "getting people to buy my product" to "describing features and benefits." When I clarify for my audience that I am not asking about marketing, advertising, or lead generation, our conversation begins to move in a fairly predictable direction. I usually ask my audience to reduce their answers to verbs, and that's when it gets interesting. Remember the original question: "What is sales?" Below is a sample of the verbs that pertain to selling:

to persuade	to teach
to advise	to entertain
to influence	to guide
to "close"	to convince
to relate	to educate
to inform	to assist
to consult	to help

When we represent a product or service, we take on many of the roles above. We teach, advise, persuade, relate, and entertain. Most importantly, we help. This is the word I want to focus on, as I believe "to help" is at the very heart of any ethical sales situation. If my primary goal is to help my client, then I must be able to understand the need or desire that underlies my products' value proposition. In simpler terms, what are all the possible ways in which my product or service will be helpful to my client?

When I speak of entertaining a client, it is in the same context as entertaining a guest, rather than performing or putting on a show. Entertaining a client means welcoming them and making them comfortable. By focusing on the experience and reducing, sometimes even eliminating, the barrier to trust, we enter a helpful role, rather than an adversarial one. Our goal is to create a consultative and experiential relationship.

The most frustrating moments in the sales process are usually the result of a client's lack of understanding of what would be most helpful for them. In all but the simplest transactions, ensuring the client's clear understanding requires the salesperson to be mindful of "the big picture," rather than only having a micro-view. Due to a limited understanding of our solutions, a client may ask a simple initial question which they believe is the most important factor. If we answer this basic question, our customer may make a poor decision based on this single piece of information. This may prompt the client to terminate the conversation prematurely. They disengage and we've lost our ability to realize our client's actual goals. I am not inferring clients are unaware, uneducated or confused. I am saying, in many cases, our clients just don't have a full grasp of our overall value proposition. The following is a typical scenario:

1. Our customer asks a basic question
2. We answer the question
3. Our customer disengages based on this single piece of information
4. We've lost our ability to help them realize their true goals.

We must become adept at discovering the true goals and needs of our clients rather than taking the "presenting need" at face value and running with it. This is the difference between, "I had to make some adjustments to the solution, but they are very happy with the results," and "It's not my fault, I sold them what they asked for." What our clients are asking for is not always the best product or solution to satisfy their deeper need. It's up to us to discover this deeper need before we help them move forward.

When we are the customers and not the salespeople, can we possibly have in-depth understanding and expertise regarding every product or service we purchase? Of course, we can't. To put this into perspective, let's look at some of the typical questions clients ask in different sales situations:

- What is your lowest interest rate for a refinance?
- What is the efficiency rating for this dryer?
- How much is the copay?
- How fast can you sell my home?
- What's the discount if I order in bulk?
- What's your best price on the full package?

- What is your lowest monthly premium for $100k-worth of life insurance?

Let's examine that first question about a refinance through the eyes of a mortgage loan officer:

Terri the new mortgage loan officer

Terri began her career as a loan officer for a mortgage brokerage just 30 days ago. Prior to her new position, she was a title clerk for the local title company. While she was familiar with the mortgage industry, she was new to the loan origination portion of the process. She completed several weeks of training regarding the different types of loans her employer offered, she learned the software system, and she mastered the loan qualification process. Terri is feeling extremely comfortable with the technical aspects of her position and she's always considered herself to be a "people person." With regard to sales, Terri received some basic sales advice and was told not to be shy when asking for the sale.

Today, Terri received her company certification and will begin receiving mortgage leads for the first time. She has a 90-day guarantee, and she knows mortgages can take some time to process and close. She is excited to get some loans in the pipeline. Her boss gave her a quick pep talk and told her that the first prospect was coming her way.

While Terri is organizing her desk and workspace, the phone rings. Terri knows the call is being transferred to her because someone has asked about a mortgage. With a little excitement, Terri answers:

"Thank you for holding, this is Terri. How can I help you?"

"Hi," the caller says, "can you tell me what your best rate is on a refinance, please?"

"Sure," Terri responds, wanting to show that she has a handle on things. "Let me just take a look at the rate sheets."

Finding the lowest rate on the sheet for a refinance, she tells the customer, "It looks like the lowest rate right now is 5.25%." Because Terri knows the best way to get going is to fill out the loan application, she asks, "Do you have time to go through the application process with me?"

"No thanks, not right now," the prospective customer says. "I want to make a few more calls before I go down that road. Thanks for your time."

"OK," thanks for calling," Terri says without much enthusiasm.

Terri is reflecting on the call when her manager pops up at her cubicle and asks, "How'd it go?"

"Not great," she says, "he just wanted to know what our best rate for a refi was, and I couldn't get him to fill out an application with me."

"OK," says the manager. "Next time try to find out more about the customer's situation and get them involved in a conversation. Make sure you ask for the sale!"

"Alright," Terri responds, not quite sure what to do differently. "I'll give it a try."

As the day progresses, Terri takes a few more phone calls and follows up with a list of "old prospects" her boss gave her. She does complete one application and she's hopeful that a couple of other people she spoke with might turn into something; she's starting to wonder if she's doing something wrong. She's been answering customers' questions as helpfully as possible, but when she asks if they want to apply, most of them say something like, "Not right now." *I've got to try something different*, she keeps thinking to herself. What Terri is dealing with is not uncommon in sales situations. I would wager that thousands of salespeople struggle with this issue every day.

Let's consider the customer's side of things. Why is a prospective client asking, "Can you tell me what your best rate is on a refinance, please?" You might believe they are attempting to get the "best deal" or the lowest possible monthly payment. In many cases, however, the client simply doesn't know there are multiple differentiating factors when comparing refinance mortgages. They believe the most important factor is the interest rate, so they use this as a comparison-shopping tool. They might call several mortgage companies, asking the same question, and then choose to apply with the company that has the lowest rate.

This approach sounds practical, doesn't it? Now imagine a scenario in which the customer chooses a particular mortgage because they were quoted a lower interest rate, only to find out they won't qualify for that mortgage because of some other factor. Even worse, let's assume they qualify, sign and close the mortgage for a lower mortgage payment, but their deeper need was to better their overall financial situation and reduce their monthly payments as much as possible. With the "rate and term" loan they received with the best interest rate, they were unable to payoff other credit card and installment debt. In addition, there may be other factors in determining "helpfulness" to this client.

Telling the customer what the "lowest rate for a refinance" is, without knowing what their overall goal is, or whether they will potentially qualify for that loan, is somewhat meaningless. Our potential customer is simply unaware of the complexities, so they mentally simplify the shopping experience by focusing on what they believe is the most important factor. In reality, there are many factors to consider. Here are some factors and considerations involved when trying to answer the simple "best rate" question:

- Interest rate
- Size of loan
- Fixed rate or adjustable rate
- Combined loan-to-value considerations (How much will this mortgage allow the client to borrow against the home?)
- Rate and term or "cash out" abilities (Can the client pay off the existing mortgage and other debt such as installment loans and credit cards?)
- Tax implications of the new loan versus the client's current situation
- Overall loan term (in years)
- The client's future plans
- Lending guidelines and credit requirements
- Mortgage "points," fees and other costs

It would have been so much easier had the customer understood the complexity involved and asked better questions, but that happens only rarely. The majority of customers ask about rates, perhaps because they believe the interest rate is the one piece of information they need to compare options and decide how to move forward.

Has there ever been a potential mortgage client who has said, "Hello, I would like to know your best possible solution for a cash-out, debt consolidation refinance, given the fact that I am in a 37% tax bracket, currently, have a combined loan to value of 72%, my home is worth exactly $550,000 and I am a self-employed contractor. I have an adjusted gross income of $140,000 per year and a debt to income ratio of 42%. Furthermore, I have $200,000 of unencumbered assets, I plan to stay in this home for another 13 years or more. I have $27,000 of credit card and installment loans that I would like to pay-off, and my credit score is 684. By the way, I'm a Virgo and I love a good cabernet."

Coming into contact with a client who is this knowledgeable and prepared is exceedingly rare. Having said this, it is also important for us to give our customers credit for their level of knowledge and understanding. If a mortgage customer *does* come in as prepared as this, don't start with, "So, let's start from the beginning, you want to borrow against your home?"

In my experience, many of the questions consumers typically ask focus on only one factor (either price, payment, discount, term, time to delivery, etc.). It's our job to find out if this factor will satisfy the deeper need of our client.

What does this mean? This means that salespeople who want to be most helpful for their clients must learn how to take control of the sales process. We must be able to explain and simplify this complexity in an effort to show our client the best road forward. Due to the complexity inherent in the vast majority of sales situations, we must become a guide for our clients; we must seek to understand their overall goals before we provide information and advice.

It is important for us to see ourselves as consultants, rather than salespeople. As consultative sales professionals, we are either helping our customers solve problems or satisfy desires (and sometimes both). The next time someone asks you what you do for a living, say, "I'm a problem-solving desire satisfier." Put it on your business card, if nothing else, it will be a great conversation starter at happy hour!

CONSULTATIVE SALES

How do we begin to help our customers reach their ultimate goals unless we know what those goals are? How can we provide a price, payment, term, rate, or technical detail when we don't yet know if that single piece of information has value for this particular customer? The answer is, we can't. We shouldn't. Let's take another look at the list of typical customer questions:

- What is your lowest interest rate for a refinance?
- What is the efficiency rating for this dryer?
- How much is the copay?
- How fast can you sell my home?
- What's the discount if I order in bulk?
- What's your best price on the full package?
- What is your lowest monthly premium for $100k-worth of life insurance?

Would answering any of these questions be helpful to reach the customer's ultimate goal? The answer is, "Maybe, maybe not."

- Dryers with the best efficiency ratings often take longer to dry and have a smaller capacity
- I could sell your home in a day if I put it on the market for half of its value.
- You can have a minimal copay if you accept a huge deductible.
- You want the lowest monthly premium on life insurance? Sure, just take a one-year term policy. Your price will go up as you age, and you'll end up spending much more on life insurance (assuming you live), but that's not what was asked here.

A salesperson might provide a rate, payment, price, term, quote, or detail – and then sell you that price, payment, or feature for all they are worth. A consultant, on the other hand, will help the customer understand the complexity involved, while also discovering the customer's real goals and the details of their situation. In actual consultative situations, it's quite evident that the "consultant" must take the lead in the conversation. Consider the following examples:

- The first question from the defendant to their defense attorney, "Do you think I should go with an insanity defense?"
- The first question from a patient to their primary care physician, "Hey doc, my toe hurts, do you think I'll need surgery?"
- The first question to an accountant, "I'm forming a new company, should I go with an LLC or C Corp?"

In all of these situations, the professional has to take the lead and learn more about the customer's goals before they can provide advice. Can you imagine the doctor saying, "yes, let's schedule surgery for Tuesday," without asking a single question or doing any examination and diagnosis? I don't know about you, but I'd hobble right out of there as quickly as I could.

The point is, to be most helpful we must take control of the dialogue and guide our customers forward through the sales process. ***Authentic selling, in all but the simplest of situations, is a consultative process***. Consultative selling requires that we learn as we advise, we understand as we inform, and we persuade our customers to take action only in the pursuit of their overall goals. If we do this while providing a positive and transparent experience, the potential value of our products and services increases exponentially.

When we seek professional advice, we instinctively fall into the pattern of allowing the expert to take control. As we seek guidance or information from a doctor, lawyer, accountant, or other professional, we state our initial problem or situation. We then expect them to begin the process of fully understanding our problems, our questions, and our need for information before they provide solutions and choices. Unfortunately, as consumers, we don't enter sales situations believing the salesperson is a consultative professional.

Selling is about persuading and influencing a prospective client toward a specific course of action. But consider the simplistic nature of this definition. Imagine the popcorn hawker at your local ballpark, "POPcorn here, get your hot buttered POPcorn heeere." Are they not influencing a potential course of action? Sure they are. Someone interested will ask, "How much is it?" This popcorn hawker is not a consultant, and replies, "Five dollars."

Now let's change it. The fan asks, "How much is it?"

"How many people are in your group?" asks Popcorn.

"Three."

"Great!" says Popcorn, "Then I'd recommend three. They're five bucks each, but I can give you three for twelve. You'll save three bucks, and you won't have to share yours."

"Sounds good," says the fan. "I'll take three, here's fifteen, keep the change!"

Now, this is a popcorn consultant! They provided advice and made a recommendation based on information unique to this customer's situation. Our "consultant" also offered an incentive to follow the recommendation, (and received a $3 tip!).

I intentionally used a simple example to show how even the most basic of sales conversations provides us with the opportunity to leap over the boundaries of sales and step into the realm of consulting. Let's examine how Terri, from earlier in this chapter, could have used this.

Terri the mortgage loan officer, continued

The caller asks Terri,

"Can you tell me what your best rate is on a refinance, please?"

"Absolutely," says Terri, "there are several different types of refinance loans. Can you tell me a little more about what you're trying to accomplish? Why are you considering a refinance of your mortgage?"

"Well," says the customer, "I have an adjustable-rate now that's climbing. I want to get into a fixed rate and hopefully lower my payments."

"I'd love to help you do that," says Terri. "Are you looking to improve your overall financial situation, or stick to just your mortgage itself?"

Can you imagine where this conversation could go now? If Terri maintains the lead in this conversation, she will gather the information she needs for her application, and she will be in a much better position to reach the customer's actual goals. With this approach, making a recommendation and providing advice to her customer will be much more meaningful (and successful).

When we choose to consult rather than sell, we elevate our standing with the customer; we perform at a higher level; we are much more successful at achieving the deeper needs of our clients; and we take more pride in what we do for a living. Executed with professionalism, integrity, and well-aligned intentions, sales is a noble, helpful, and rewarding endeavor.

Key Takeaways – Chapter One

- Professional selling is an advisory process. It is a process of helping.
- The assistance we provide should always be in service to our customer.
- The sales professional must lead the conversation.

CHAPTER TWO
SELLING IN A DIGITAL WORLD

"The most significant barrier to understanding the value of human expertise is the perception of simplicity."

EVERYTHING IS "GOING DIGITAL"

While *The Sales Upgrade* applies to all sales: digital, analog, or otherwise, it would be ludicrous not to recognize the impact of modern digital solutions on sales environments and processes. This chapter is meant to provide an overview of the online sales environment as well as my thoughts on how we, as humans, continue to provide value throughout the sales process. Even if your organization, products, and services are not currently affected by online solutions, this chapter will provide you with a full understanding of the value of interacting with a human being during the sales process.

Billions of dollars are being spent every year on "digital business transformation." This investment in technology and infrastructure is a proactive attempt to prepare for the future and a reaction to the changing demands and habits of consumers. Over the past few years, there has been a grand reversal. When digital solutions were first designed, they were created to enhance our analog solutions. Today, we are reengineering our analog processes to enhance our digital solutions. As organizations and individuals, we must embrace digital parity. Our analog processes and our digital processes must combine into a single, coordinated, modern retail process.

The availability of information online, the ability to transact remotely, and shortened "time to gratification" have all come together with other factors to push consumers and businesses further down the digital road. What percentage of your customers have looked at comparisons, done some research, or obtained information online? These new solutions provide tremendous value and convenience to our customers on a daily basis. Many salespeople are asking, "Am I going to be replaced?"

The Need for Human Beings

In spite of all the advances in digital, artificial intelligence (AI), and modern technology, in sales situations there are still four things computers and digital solutions just can't do. They can't relate to us on a human level; they can't provide a tailored or customized experience; they can't use expertise and experience to provide genuine advice; and they can't negotiate price in a variable price environment. As complexity increases, the need for human involvement also increases. Digital solutions begin to falter as situations become more complex. *The most significant barrier to understanding the value of human expertise is the perception of simplicity.* Let's dig a little deeper into each of these:

Computers and digital solutions can't relate to us on a human level

They do not share our human existence, and regardless of what you've seen in the movies, they cannot make a human connection. If I was to share with a computer that I'd love to take a vacation to the Bahamas, the software couldn't honestly say it would also like to take a vacation. It couldn't tell me that's it's been to the Bahamas before and share with me a cherished family memory from it's childhood. The computer couldn't tell me about a favorite restaurant it visited. It could certainly provide information about the most popular places to go, but it simply could not create any human rapport.

There is no doubt that sophisticated AI bots could be programmed to say these things to a consumer, but they would be obvious lies. I'm not sure about your thoughts on the matter, but being lied to by a computer program to gain my trust gives me the heebie-jeebies.

Digital solutions cannot provide a tailored or customized experience

A significant advantage of digital solutions is consistency. They operate the same way based on a set of instructions they follow. This creates another disadvantage because computer programs are somewhat unable to consider a unique human situation and change their programming for that one situation. Computers are only able to make an "exception" if they have been programmed to do so. Once a computer is programmed to make an exception for a particular circumstance, it ceases to be an exception. It will then behave the same way under these circumstances every time.

While this might seem like a great feature, it creates an environment ripe for manipulation. I once heard a woman at an airport whispering expletives into her phone (go ahead and imagine that for a moment). I thought she was utterly bonkers, and I couldn't help but ask, "Is everything ok?" She replied, "Oh, yeah, sorry you had to hear that. I've learned that the phone system for the airline will transfer me to a real person if I swear." While I understand why the system was programmed to function this way, the result is a manipulatable process that is anything but tailored or customized.

Computerized solutions cannot provide human-to-human advice

They can look at statistical facts and provide information, but that is far from guidance and advice. Using the example from above, if I asked a computer whether I should go to the Bahamas or the Mediterranean, what information might it provide? The AI might provide statistics to show the most popular destination or scan reviews to see which destination gets higher ratings. If the system is sophisticated, it might ask questions about family size, the age of family members, and whether we prefer indoor or outdoor activities. It would then use some algorithm to steer us toward one destination or the other.

Would we accept the analytical determination of this computer? I believe most of us would rather speak to a human being who has personally been to both locations or someone who has helped many families put together their vacations, someone who has heard the stories and details of these vacations. Computers can provide information, but information does not equal advice.

Computers cannot negotiate price in a variable price environment

In situations where price is negotiable and variable, digital solutions fail for two reasons. First, these solutions cannot tailor the pricing to the situation. This is remarkably similar to the issues with providing a tailored or customized experience. Once the computer has been programmed to give a specific price based on particular circumstances, the price ceases to be variable. This system allows us to manipulate the computer into providing the lowest price possible. The second reason variable pricing fails in digital environments is due to human nature.

Negotiation is a process of discovering what's best for both buyer and seller. When the computer gives us the best price, is it really the best price? Digital sales platforms have better success rates when "the price is the price" and there are no exceptions. When we know we can negotiate the price, we won't be inclined to accept the numbers given by the computer.

An excellent example of this is Carvana, an online used car retailer. One of the best examples of negotiable variable pricing is arguably the used car market. With their non-negotiable flat pricing, Carvana has created an online digital platform for used cars. I doubt this would have been possible if they would have maintained a model where prices were negotiable.

THE NEW PATH FOR SALES PROFESSIONALS

On the positive side, as price and quality diminish as a deciding factor, the customer experience becomes even more critical. On the negative side, for some sales organizations, the best experience is one where there is no human involvement. This is why customers are moving further and further down the digital path. We absolutely must create an enjoyable, value-added, customer-centric path for our potential clients to follow.

As this trend continues to spread within sales organizations, sales professionals will be required to learn new skills, adapt to new realities, and continue to differentiate their products and services on a human level. The difficulty for most organizations will not be technology and infrastructure; it will be human behavior. As I stated above, there are some things computers and digital solutions just can't do. Your success may very well hinge on your ability to bridge this gap and bring parity to your digital and analog processes. Your customer's experience cannot be compromised by a lack of coordination.

Many organizations achieving success in this modern digital landscape are providing three separate paths for their customers. I've labeled these paths Traditional, Digital, and Modern.

The Traditional Path

Right smack dab in the middle of this ever-changing digital landscape, there are still those customers who want to move through the process in a traditional way. This might be due to an existing relationship with one of the sales professionals, or merely a desire to do it the way they've done it in the past.

These customers may have done some research online, but they didn't initiate any digital exchange with you. In spite of modern online alternatives, furniture stores continue to operate in this space quite successfully. Consumers want to see, feel, and interact with these products physically. They want to sit on the couch, open the dresser drawers, and see how *this* lamp goes with *that* rug. This path will continue to shrink as a more substantial part of the population moves toward digital solutions.

The Digital Path

These are customers that investigate, initiate, negotiate, and transact in an entirely digital environment. As stated previously in this chapter, this is most valuable (and most common), in an environment where products and services are simple rather than complex, human connection and expertise are unnecessary, and prices are not variable or negotiable.

The simplest example of this is Amazon. More complex cases exist, and there may still be human interaction, but this interaction won't be by phone or in person. The communication between your team members and customers would be entirely digital. Imagine you are investigating the purchase of a new laptop online. On your own, you narrow it down to a few choices. Eventually, you think you've chosen the right one, but you want to be sure it does what you think it does, and comes with what you think it should. You hit the "Chat with an expert" button on the website and ask your questions via live chat. With your questions answered, you complete the transaction online. For all you know, the person you "chatted" with could have been an AI Bot.

The Modern Path

The modern approach is a hybrid environment. Parts of the investigation, initiation, negotiation, and transaction are digital, and parts of the process are analog, real-time conversations by phone or in person with another human being. This hybrid system allows consumers the convenience of gathering information, making choices, and communicating digitally on their terms. Also, they can leverage a human connection, as well as human experience and expertise to make decisions and reduce stress. In this environment, your customer may move back and forth between a digital experience and a human experience, providing the best of both worlds. This is the fastest-growing segment and where I believe the most significant opportunity presents itself.

Fighting to claim their place in the new digital world, many organizations have created a digital path for their customers in addition to the established traditional route. Afterward, they've expressed frustration when these paths are not teeming with digital customers, marching right through a completed transaction. I believe the reason for this is the lack of digital parity. As their customers move from digital to human due to complexity, price negotiation, or the need for human expertise, they are passed off to the traditional path, and they reject it. These customers have investigated your resources online, initiated contact, provided information, and potentially already made some decisions. They don't want to start all over again with your traditional path, circa 1982. This is why we need a modern hybrid approach. As your customer moves from digital to human and back again, respect the choices they've already made, give credit to the information they've already provided, and continue down the path they want to go. They will love you for it.

Unfortunately, where some organizations have created a digital path, they've gotten the people side of this equation wrong. Some companies have created the correct paths, but they've staffed them with sales teams often operating in separate silos. What happens when a customer starts in the traditional route and later goes online and initiates communication with your "digital retail department?" What happens when a customer begins contact with your team digitally and then moves to the traditional path? It's not uncommon for a customer to move through these two paths simultaneously. Separated in their silos, you now have two salespeople from the same company competing against each other. As chaos ensues, value creation suffers, the customer experience goes down the tubes, and profit margins disappear. Everyone loses.

We don't need traditional salespeople and digital salespeople. We need modern sales professionals who can move through all three paths as necessary based on their customer's preferences. Where three paths existed, only one remains - the modern path. If you are more traditional, embrace digital. If you see yourself as a digital sales professional, embrace the human component. The conventional approach is slowly fading as new generations embrace new alternatives. The digital approach is incomplete and limited in most complex sales situations. The modern approach allows us to adapt and pivot between analog and digital processes as our customers fluidly navigate through awareness, consideration, education negotiation, transaction, and acquisition. For many organizations, the question, "where are we going?" has already been answered. The difficulty is figuring out how to get there from where we are now.

For all of these reasons, the behaviors and skillsets of successful sales professionals are changing. To direct and incentivize these changes in our processes and actions, many organizations will make changes to our reward systems and pay structures. To best prepare yourself and continue to succeed in sales, I recommend fully immersing yourself in a well-rounded approach. You will future-proof your skillset and continue to flourish as you help your customers navigate between the digital and the analog.

TRANSPARENCY AND COMPLEXITY

As consumers now have fast and easy access to a great deal of information online, transparency has become extremely important. It's ok to allow your customers to see inside your sales process and understand how things will move forward. As I discussed previously, the more complex a sales transaction becomes, the more human interaction is required to finalize decisions, avoid errors, and reduce stress. As you move between digital and human interactions with your customers, transparency and complexity will both be extremely useful. In fact, I suggest you be extremely transparent about the complexity.

Revealing Complexity

The more complex the situation is, the more the customer needs you to help them navigate it. This increases the value you add to the transaction, so *be transparent about the complexity*. Things are not always as simple as we believe they are. Consider the following example that happened to my friend.

So, my "friend" (let's call him John), had issues with his garbage disposal. John decided to replace his garbage disposal by himself. John watched a YouTube video on how to remove the old one and replace it with a new one. It looked simple enough. To purchase the new one, he went straight to Amazon. John reviewed available options, saw the pricing, read reviews, and ultimately decided on a unit a little more powerful than his current one. Two days later, the new disposal arrived. John removed the old one fairly quickly and, with confidence, began to install the new one. It didn't fit.

Due to the larger size of the unit, the disposal couldn't be installed without having to reconfigure the plumbing pipes. John had to return the new unit, incurring inconvenience as well as shipping fees. Since John had already removed the old disposal, he needed a new one immediately. He went to his local home improvement store, and working with one of the helpful employees, John selected a disposal with the correct dimensions, (he brought the old one with him). The employee also informed him that he would need plumber's putty to complete the installation without leaks. An hour later, it was installed and working.

As simple as they might seem, digital solutions by themselves cannot always solve our problems. I (I mean, John), learned this the hard way. When you engage with a customer, it's a good practice to share transparent information about your previous experiences, which reveal the complexity involved in what otherwise might seem simple. This increases your value, enhances the consumer experience, and reduces future inconvenience and stress for your customer.

A Word on Price Transparency

When the price is quite different between competitors, it becomes a significant decision factor. Divulging price under these circumstances can create a decision point before the customer understands the full value. In this situation, steering the customer away from the price until they have experienced and understood the total value is a win for both parties. In simpler terms, this helps consumers know what they are getting for what they are paying. This also helps sales professionals succeed when their prices are higher, and their value proposition warrants a higher price.

When price and quality are similar, price ceases to be the decision factor. In this circumstance, early transparency with pricing can be a competitive advantage. Since price is much less likely to be the decision factor, our early and honest explanation of pricing reduces stress and friction, enhancing the consumer experience. Digital transactions are easier to facilitate as prices flatten, and price differentiation is minimized. Based on your environment and competitive landscape, you can determine whether or not either of these strategies will work for you. I provide a much more in-depth look at dealing with price considerations when I introduce you to the NAVIGATE Price model in Chapter Nine.

Before You Move On

I don't want you to leave this chapter believing this book is about "digital selling." It is, and it isn't. *The Sales Upgrade* is a book about sales techniques and behaviors. I wrote this chapter to provide an understanding of how to apply these strategies to a modern retail environment. However, *The Seven Rs of Selling*, and the other models you will learn, apply to any consultative sales environment. The next chapter will discuss the responsibilities we carry as sales professionals. After that, we'll dive into The Consultative Sales Framework in Part Two.

Key Takeaways – Chapter Two

- Digital retail solutions are impacting sales organizations *today*.
- Sales professionals must overcome the customer's perception of simplicity.
- A modern, combined sales environment must be embraced and supported.

CHAPTER THREE
SALES RESPONSIBILITIES

"Allowing a long-term view to significantly influence our actions, attitudes, and behaviors is something we owe ourselves, our customers, and our employers."

WE HAVE A RESPONSIBILITY TO OUR CUSTOMERS

When we assume the role of a consultant, we find ourselves in a position of power. We have an ethical and moral responsibility if we are to provide advice, make recommendations, and guide our customers toward a product or solution that helps them achieve their goals. In most sales situations we benefit directly from the customer's purchase of our products and solutions. This truth amplifies our need to use our expertise, combined with our persuasion and influence in service to, and for the benefit of our customer. If we do so with a genuine concern for the customer's well-being and the achievement of their goals, this will differentiate us and elevate our position. *We* become one of the reasons for our customer to choose our products and services over those of our competitors.

We are responsible for being ethical and "doing the right thing." This allows us to distance ourselves from the various negative stigmas associated with sales and salespeople. Just because you can "sell an anchor to a drowning man" doesn't mean you should. Take the high road and throw him a life preserver (and then sell him some swimming lessons).

Taking the moral high road as a salesperson is not always the easiest approach. However, viewed through a longer lens, I believe it is the best (and only) long-term approach toward a successful and rewarding career in sales. When we accept that we are consultants, we embrace this responsibility and take professional pride in exercising our power appropriately. Consider a doctor who recommends, and then performs, a surgery that is unnecessary; or consider a lawyer who recommends unnecessary litigation in pursuit of more billable hours. We should all consider such behaviors reprehensible and unconscionable. In the world of consultative sales, there is no product or service so small as to be immune to this basic ethical requirement.

One of my first sales positions was as a loan officer (and collections agent) for a consumer finance company. We did small consumer loans of $1,500 to $5,000. I was also licensed to sell insurance to our customers. We offered fire and casualty insurance on personal property, as well as life and disability insurance. These insurance products were optional.

In California, where I worked at the time, we were operating under a stipulated judgment, which required us to read a disclosure statement during the closing of the loan in the presence of the customer. Furthermore, we were required to record this on a micro cassette recorder (yes, I'm dating myself here). Why all these requirements? Well, it seems that prior to my tenure with the company, it was somewhat common to bundle the insurances into the loan and tell consumers that all the insurances were "included" or required to obtain the loan. A consumer who came to borrow $2,500 left with a loan of $2,900, personal property insurance and a $25,000 life and disability policy. Many of them didn't even know they had the insurance.

I can still remember the disclosure all these years later, "You understand that the insurance products we offer are optional and are not required to obtain your loan…"

We were still very successful selling these insurances, but we did it with full disclosure, which meant we had to focus on the value proposition. Most of the loans we completed were secured against personal property. Insuring that property was a good move for most consumers. In a negative situation, they could lose their property to fire, theft, or earthquake and still have to pay back the loan. Home and auto lenders can and do require insurance on the asset securing the loan. Due to the indirect relationship between the personal property and the loan, we weren't able to require it, but that didn't render it less valuable to a consumer who understood this complexity. In the San Francisco earthquake of 1989, many of our customers suffered loss of personal property. Those who were insured were able to either pay off the loan or replace their property. Unfortunately, those who weren't insured began defaulting at a much higher rate. They were tasked with making a loan payment for property they no longer had, while at the same time spending money to recover from earthquake damages.

We have a responsibility to take the long-term view. **Allowing a long-term view to significantly influence our actions, attitudes, and behaviors is something we owe ourselves, our customers, and our employers.** It is too easy in any sales position to take a short-term view, boosting sales and commissions in the near term while sacrificing your own personal brand. In addition you risk damaging the reputation of the company and your relationship with your customer. This applies to the promises we make and the expectations we create during the sales process.

An example of this is a prominent bank in the not-so-distant past where sales teams were achieving their sales targets by opening accounts for customers without necessity or permission. In the short term, quotas were achieved; sales teams reached bonuses and increased commissions. In the long term, the company's reputation suffered mightily and the stock price took a huge hit (and is yet to fully recover). While this is a macro view, there are plenty of examples at the micro-level, including:

- A contractor including a $2500 allowance for kitchen countertops to make their price look lower, when the cost of the countertops will likely be closer to $7500.
- An appliance salesperson recommending a brand due to the "spiff" the manufacturer is offering rather than the product that would truly be best for their customer.
- A real estate agent promising they will be heavily involved and working hard to sell your home, then disappearing as soon as you sign the listing agreement.
- Any salesperson promising an unachievable delivery date to gain the sale.

In all of these cases, a "sale" might be achieved. However, it is unlikely that this customer will do business with this company (and especially this individual) again. If you consider your own experiences, you will likely find other examples of this.

If you have a thorough understanding of your products and services, and how they provide a benefit for your customers, there is no need to "trick" a customer into purchasing them. All viable products and services have a value proposition, and we are responsible for conveying that understanding to our clients with full disclosure and transparency. Our approach should be free of falsehoods, misrepresentation, or hidden agendas. Through my eyes, if you need to rely on these unethical practices to be successful, either you need to improve your consultative selling skills, or you need to find more valuable products and services to represent.

Having said this, I also believe there are methods and strategies involved in the timing of disclosure. Ostensibly, there are advantages in choosing your products and services. The manner and order of presentation and disclosure will influence the customer's decision. If you handle this incorrectly, you do yourself, your customer, and your employer a disservice. As an example, many customers ask us, "How much is it?" before they understand the full value of our offering. This could potentially lead the customer to make a premature decision based on price alone. This isn't good for them or us. It's almost always better to discuss the full offering in detail prior to discussing price. When and how information is revealed is extremely important, as we shall see in future chapters.

We are responsible for honoring the customer's values. One of the most common errors in sales is losing sight of the customer's value system. This occurs most often when we project our own value system on to our client. As salespeople, we are often working with clients who are in a different situation than we are. I've often worked with salespeople who have a range of products or services and for whatever reason, they are unable or unwilling to sell (or even offer) certain products and services to their clients. An example of this might be an automotive service advisor who does not routinely offer extended warranty coverage to a client. When explored, the advisor says, "Why would anyone want that? Most people get a new car every three years anyway." This is a clear indication that the salesperson is projecting their own value system on to the client.

Additionally, many times the difference between salespeople and their customers has to do with the overall value and price. Many salespeople have a hard time justifying the price of products and services that they would not purchase themselves.

WE HAVE A RESPONSIBILITY TO OUR EMPLOYER

In addition to handling our clients and customers responsibly, we have an obligation to represent our employer to the best of our ability and maximize the value of every sale (within the constraints previously discussed). This responsibility requires us to be professional, diligent, and knowledgeable. Let's look at these one at a time:

We are responsible for being professional. Showing up as a professional everyday is not as easy as it sounds. There are many elements to this and all must be maintained to get this right. To our customers, we are often the face of the company and they will take their cues from us. This means we have a high bar to uphold - from the way we dress to the way we speak about our products, services, facilities, policies and coworkers. Consider these statements:

- "I don't know why they still have this product; nobody buys it."
- "They don't really know what they're doing in that department, I'm sorry you had to deal with that."
- "I'm sorry, if it was up to me, I'd let you do it, but that's their policy."
- "Yeah, we've needed a new coat of paint for a while. I keep telling them but they're not listening."
- "They didn't tell me you were coming in today; they do that all the time."

In all of these cases, we've crossed the barrier into unprofessionalism. In so doing we've made our company, our products, our services, and our reputation less valuable to this consumer. In many cases, we say such things to build ourselves up and separate ourselves from something negative. Try counting the number of times the words "they, their and them" are used. What we fail to realize is that "they, their, and them," is actually, "I, we, ours, and us." There are always better ways to communicate with our customers without painting a poor picture of our company, coworkers, or products. Let's take another look at those statements through these eyes:

- "It's not sold at a high volume, but it's a quality product and we like to maintain a good variety."
- "Let me coordinate with that department and get all the details. We'll do our best to help."
- "Let me see what we can do to help you."
- "I'll make a note of it. We appreciate your feedback."
- "Welcome! I wasn't expecting you, what a great surprise!"

Did you see the transformation when we used, "I, me, and we?" When we embrace the idea that we are not an island unto ourselves, and accept that we are part of the whole, we understand that our role as a professional expands way beyond the dress code. If you find that you are emotionally or mentally just not in the right place, take a breather and hit the reset button. I discuss this more in Part 3 (Chapter 14) when we tackle the topic of 'Self Awareness.'

In addition to the way you dress, and the way you speak to your customers, part of being a professional is following through on your commitments and doing what you say you will do. If you tell a customer you will work up a quote or get back to them with details, then you had better do it when you said you would (or before!). If you are a homeowner and have ever worked with contractors, you know exactly what I am talking about. In my experience, this is the best example of exactly what *not* to do. Many individuals are exceptionally good at what they do, but simply lack good follow-up skills. It is worth developing good habits in this area because it can be a tremendously beneficial differentiating factor. When my wife and I finally find a painter, handyman, landscaper, or other contractor who follows up on time, shows up when they tell us they will, and completes work when they say they will, we are happy to give them our business and pay a premium.

This concept also extends to doing what our organization or employer says we will do. This requires us to be aware of our sales literature, product brochures and our clients' expectations. Each client's experience is a huge part of the sales process and our ability to deliver this experience consistently and professionally gives us an excellent competitive advantage. You are responsible for keeping the promises your organization makes. If not you, who?

We are responsible for doing the whole job, not just the parts we want to do. In many cases, sales team members are not only responsible for the initial sale, but also for maintaining a long-term relationship with the customer. This benefits the salesperson as an individual, assuming they will remain with the company into the future. It also benefits the employer, as it strengthens the relationship with the customer and elevates the overall value proposition. I have run across countless examples of sales teams and individuals who focus entirely on new sales rather than on taking care of their existing customer base; sacrificing repeat and referral business for immediate conquest sales. Regardless of how long an individual salesperson plans to work with this employer or represent these specific products and services, we owe it to our employer to "do the whole job." This approach includes following up with our client base and providing those services and "extras" our employer reasonably asks of us, and our customers expect. There is nothing you can do that is more productive in the long term.

Doing the whole job also extends to the idea of introducing customers to the full line of products and services on offer. I often encounter salespeople who narrowly sell only certain product or service offerings and don't even mention other available offerings. One of the worst things to hear a customer say is, "Oh, I didn't know you guys offered that, we just agreed to do that with _____!" (Fill in the blank with your biggest competitor). To accomplish this, we simply have to be proactive about introducing our customers to the full breadth of products and services we offer: "I know you are here for _____ today, but I wanted to make sure you were aware of _____ for future consideration."

We are responsible for maintaining up-to-date knowledge of the products and services offered by our company. This increases our value as a consultant to the customer and provides us with the ability to build value and justify price. Staying up to date has become more difficult with shortened product lifecycles, technological advances and rapid software updates, but this has made it that much more important. If your product line is so large that there is no possible way to be an expert on everything, at least know how to use available resources to represent the product correctly and answer customer questions in a timely fashion. Do your best to stay up to date with your industry and your competitors.

WE HAVE A RESPONSIBILITY TO OURSELVES

Our most important responsibility is to ourselves. When we embark on a career in sales, we owe it to ourselves to make it personally rewarding. We should be able to take pride in what we do and how we do it.

We are entitled to feel good about what and whom we are representing. Sales can be so much more rewarding when we believe in what we are selling. Spend the time to fully understand the value and competitive advantages of your products and services and convince yourself that your offerings are worth representing. If you are not comfortable representing a particular offering or feel that to do so would interfere with your own sense of morality and ethics, this is a clear indication to find other products and services to represent.

Above all, you should feel like you are helping your customers. You deserve to enjoy your work and feel like you are contributing something good to the world around you. If you don't, something is wrong.

Maximize your income

As sales professionals, we have the right to maximize our income and sell as much as we can. Sales wouldn't be the rush that it is if we couldn't increase our earnings as much as possible. As long as you don't violate your ethical responsibility and you work within the guidelines and framework created by your employer, you should feel comfortable maximizing your own income. Feel free to "knock it out of the park" on a sale, as long as you feel good about what you've accomplished for your customer. In most of the industries I've worked with, the happiest customers are those who made the largest purchases.

Adapt, learn, grow, and evolve

We are responsible for adapting, learning, growing and evolving. Whether you like it or not, you have a responsibility to yourself to continue to learn, to improve your skills and knowledge, to embrace change, and to adapt to your surrounding circumstances. If you do not, you will eventually fail. As stated in the introduction, if you believe you are peaking, and you can never be better than you currently are, you are at the beginning of the end. The world around us is in a constant state of change, and the rate of change continues to accelerate.

Ask anyone who has had a long, successful career in sales how much has changed since they first started. Ask them what would have happened if they had not adapted to these changes. Products and services have changed. The tools we use during the sales process have changed. Customer relationship management systems have changed. The methods and tools that customers use to communicate with us have changed. With the constant desire for "complete integration," everything has become more complex. In addition, many industries have seen shrinking margins due to the availability of comparison shopping tools and commoditization. In turn, this changes commission structures and earning potential.

Have you ever heard someone in sales referred to as a "relic?" The biggest difference between becoming a relic, and maintaining a very successful sales career, is your willingness to grow, learn, and adapt to change.

Key Takeaways – Chapter Three

- You have an ethical and moral responsibility to use your skills and abilities to achieve what's best for your customers.
- You are responsible for upholding your own promises as well as the promises of your employer.
- You are entitled to feel good about what you do, take pride in what you represent, and maximize your income.
- It is imperative that you embrace change, and adapt to the evolution of your sales environment.

PART TWO:

THE CONSULTATIVE SALES FRAMEWORK

CHAPTER FOUR
THE SEVEN Rs OF SELLING (R7)

"It's amazing what can happen with a little forethought and an extra 45 seconds."

THE SEVEN Rs OF SELLING

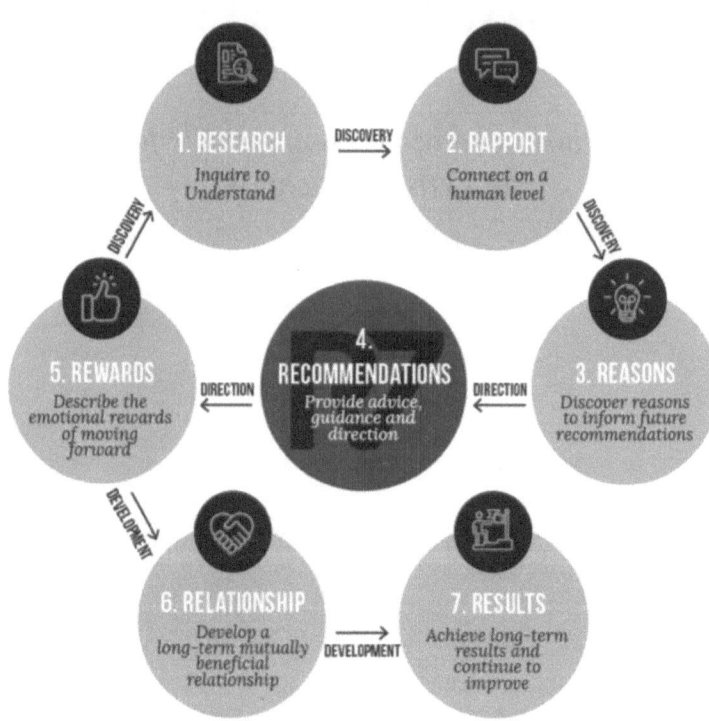

THE SEVEN Rs OF SELLING (R7)

This chapter is your first introduction to R7. As you move through it and digest the overall concept, don't be discouraged if you do not become completely comfortable with the approach or do not understand the complexity of it just yet. In Part 3 of this book (Chapters 10-14) I revisit each of the Seven Rs in much more detail, and provide different examples from multiple industries. In Part 4 of this book I will apply The Seven Rs of Selling to your unique sales environment, and guide you through the design of your own strategy.

In Chapter One I discussed the necessity to reframe your thoughts regarding what sales and selling are all about. I asked you to embrace the idea that the primary goal of selling is to help your client to the best of your ability. Once you embrace the idea that all sales situations are advisory in nature, you must then consider the order in which you move through the sales process, the questions you ask, and the language you use.

The Seven Rs of Selling is a model I created to frame a consultative and experiential sales methodology. This model makes it easier to learn, understand and implement a winning sales strategy in just about any sales environment. If you accept the fundamental premise that the primary goal of sales is to help your customers solve problems and satisfy desires, this model will help you build and improve upon your existing strategies and techniques. The Seven Rs of Selling are:

R1 **R**esearch
R2 **R**apport
R3 **R**easons
R4 **R**ecommendations
R5 **R**ewards
R6 **R**elationship
R7 **R**esults

The successful practitioner of R7 conducts **R**esearch, builds **R**apport, discovers the **R**easons necessary to make **R**ecommendations, and describes the **R**ewards of following those recommendations. If done correctly and consistently, the application of R7 leads to a long-term profitable Relationship and successful sales **Results**. Let's consider a simple example:

Jay and Tony's landscaping business

Jay and Tony went into the landscaping and hardscaping business together several years ago. They work hard and pride themselves on taking care of their customers. Over the past few years, their limited success has primarily been based on referrals. While they are both excellent at doing the work, neither of them considers themself a natural salesperson and this is often the most uncomfortable part of the job. They want to grow their business, but to do so they will have to win more clients. Yesterday, they agreed that Tony would handle the sales, as he is "better with people." Tony is contemplating this when his phone rings:

Scenario One

"Hello, this is Tony."

"Hi Tony, my name is Mark and I was referred to your company by my neighbor, Sam."

"Hi Mark, thanks for calling."

"Sure. Well, we moved in June and have been using the same company to maintain our lawn as the prior owners, but we're just not happy with them. I just called to see what you would charge us for our yard."

"OK, our rates go anywhere from $80 per month to $300 or more depending on a bunch of things. If you give me your email address, I'll send over our pricing sheet so you can see what we offer and pick the services you need."

"Great, thanks. My email is Mark@…"

Tony has made very little out of this valuable referral. The conversation centered on one variable (price). On what grounds will Mark make his decision to contract with Tony? It is probable that Mark will call other potential companies to compare prices. Some other company will have lower prices (because some other company always does!)

Tony didn't act like a consultant at all in this conversation. The potential customer was in control. This is the opposite of an advisory conversation, where the consultant takes the lead. In this conversation, Tony is a landscaper, not an advisor. While he thinks he is, he is not helping his customer to the best of his ability. In his heart, Tony wishes customers would choose his company because he and Jay care more, are more detailed, and provide a better service. How can he get potential customers to understand that? The answer? You guessed it! R7. Let's take a look at what this conversation could have sounded like.

Scenario Two

"Hello, this is Tony."

"Hi Tony, my name is Mark and I was referred to your company by my neighbor, Sam."

"Hi Mark, it's nice to meet you. Would that be Sam Jones over on Magnolia?"

"Yes, as a matter of fact, it is."

"That's great, they are a terrific family. I'll have to thank Sam for sending you my way. What can we do for you?"

"Well, we moved in June and have been using the same company to maintain our lawn as the prior owners, but we're just not happy with them. I just called to see what you would charge us for our yard."

"I'm sorry you're not happy with your yard, Mark. We'd love to help you with that, can you tell me what you're not happy with right now?"

"How much time do you have? There's a bunch of stuff. Just the other day, they broke our invisible fence for the dogs"

"That's frustrating. What kind of dogs do you have?"

"We have two labs."

"Labs are great family dogs, I had one growing up. We called him Grunter.

"Ours are Oscar and Crosby."

"Those are great names. Has the invisible fence been repaired yet?"

"No, I think the fence folks are coming tomorrow."

"That's good. Listen, since you're experiencing so many issues with your current company, I'd suggest we meet in person so I can see the yard myself and talk with you regarding our full range of services. I'm sure you want your yard to look amazing without these inconveniences and I want to be sure that we do a thorough job for you. You can also show me where the invisible fence is, so when we do move forward we won't repeat the problem you're dealing with now. It will also be great to meet you in person. I can find time at your convenience, would today or tomorrow provide a window for us to meet?"

"Tomorrow at five-thirty would work."

"Great, I know where Sam is on Magnolia, can you give me your address?"

"Sure, it's right next door to Sam at…."

In this scenario, Tony took the lead by asking questions. By assuming an advisory stance and directing the conversation, he was able to build **R**apport with the customer surrounding the neighbor, Sam, and the customer's dogs, Oscar and Crosby. Tony's research also led him to discover **R**easons to **R**ecommend an onsite face-to-face meeting. Tony then used these **R**easons along with the existing **R**apport to make a **R**ecommendation, and back that **R**ecommendation up with **R**ewards the customer will receive for following his **R**ecommendations. Tony also alluded to a future positive **R**elationship with Mark by speaking so kindly about Sam and his family. The **R**esults? Tony and Mark are now going to meet in person where they can continue to build a positive **R**elationship. Tony can put a more accurate quote together based on the layout of the yard and the "situation on the ground." Mark will have a chance to consider Tony's full range of services and his value proposition instead of being forced to make decisions solely based on price. Here are some things to consider about these two scenarios:

Scenario One
- The conversation lasted approximately 30 seconds.
- Tony asked no questions.
- The customer knows very little about Tony.
- Tony knows very little about his potential customer.
- The reason for the customer to move forward is good pricing.
- The reward for the customer to move forward is unclear.
- Tony made no recommendations and gave no guidance or advice.
- The next step for the customer is to review pricing and select services with no guidance.
- There is no next step setup for Tony.
- The relationship is heading toward a transactional nature.
- Results are questionable.

Scenario Two
- The conversation lasted approximately 75 seconds.
- Tony conducted **R**esearch. He asked six questions before he asked for the customer's address.
- The customer knows a bit about how Tony sees his customer, Sam. He also knows Tony grew up with a lab named Grunter. In addition to this, Mark perceives a level of concern and empathy from Tony surrounding the invisible fence.
- Tony knows that Mark has a broken invisible fence and two labs named Oscar and Crosby. He also knows the fence is being repaired tomorrow and that Mark lives right next door to Sam. Finally, he knows that Mark has been experiencing many issues with the existing landscape company and is really frustrated with them.
- Tony successfully built **R**apport.

There are several **R**easons for the customer to move forward in the process: the many issues they are currently experiencing, the desire to make the yard look amazing without inconveniences, and the need to show Tony where the invisible fence is.

Tony made a strong **R**ecommendation that they meet in person based on sound reasoning.

The **R**ewards for following Tony's suggestion are added convenience, a thorough job done on the yard and diminished chances of breaking the invisible fence in the future.

The next step for Tony and Mark is a face-to-face meeting where they can continue building a **R**elationship, and Tony can explain the full range of services he offers without the pressure of price.

Tony is expecting great **R**esults.

It's amazing what can happen with a little forethought and an extra 45 seconds. The beauty of R7 is in its simplicity. However, don't be lulled into stopping here. Once you grasp the very basics you can begin applying them immediately to every sales situation. However, it is also important to note that there is a strategy and a plan here. The ability to move through this process systematically does not happen by accident. To understand all of this better, I break down R7 in the next section and look at each component separately as well as how they relate to each other. The underlying simplicity will give way to a level of complexity that will surprise you.

BREAKING DOWN R7

R1 **R**esearch
R2 **R**apport
R3 **R**easons
R4 **R**ecommendations
R5 **R**ewards
R6 **R**elationship
R7 **R**esults

Consultative selling will require you to lead the conversation with your customer and, through an experiential process, help them discover their overall goals and deeper needs. We do this through **R**esearch. The essential role of a consultative individual is to give advice, guidance, and direction, which is done with **R**ecommendations. Our guidance, suggestions and advice must be based on solid **R**easons. **R**apport builds trust and safety. **R**apport reduces the sense of risk our customers feel when making crucial decisions. Consumers who trust us are much more likely to follow our **R**ecommendations!

While **R**easons support our **R**ecommendations from a logical perspective, **R**ewards provide the customer with an emotional incentive to move forward in the sales process. When we base our **R**ecommendations on solid **R**easoning and then describe the unique emotional **R**ewards of following our **R**ecommendations, we are proactively answering the customer's questions, "Why should I do this?" and "What will I get out of this?" We foster a positive and transparent **R**elationship with our customers throughout the sales process and, in many circumstances, throughout their life of ownership. Done well, and done consistently, this strategy leads to tremendous **R**esults. Let's take a look at each of the seven Rs one at a time.

RESEARCH

Let's start with the first "R," **R**esearch. **R**esearch is the practice of asking questions, learning about the client's situation, understanding their goals and inquiring to gain perspective. This phase of inquiry also establishes the consultant as the leader in the conversation. In the first scenario between Tony and Mark, how much research did Tony do? That's right, none! Tony didn't ask one question. This means that in the first scenario, the customer was in the lead. When a customer is in control of the conversation, the sales professional is viewed as an "information provider," which reduces their value as an advisor and expert. Remember that the person asking the questions is the person guiding the direction of the conversation. When we ask intelligent questions, we are also perceived as having more expertise (assuming that the questions are leading to a good place for the customer.)

Just when you might be saying to yourself, "Okay, I got this," I'm going to add another layer to this concept. Questions are also the tools we use to forward our sales strategy and process. Your questions cannot be random; however, you cannot always prepare them in advance. That may sound a bit contradictory, but if you bear with me, I will clarify this concept.

Let's take another look at an excerpt from Mark and Tony's conversation:

"I'm sorry you're not happy with your yard, Mark. We'd love to help you with that, can you tell me what you're not happy with right now?"

"How much time do you have? There's a bunch of stuff. Just the other day, they broke our invisible fence for the dogs."

"That's frustrating. What kind of dogs do you have?"

Tony had no idea prior to this call that he would be having this specific conversation, so there is no way he could prepare specific questions in advance. Tony's questions, however, are not random and are extremely strategic. Tony has been learning and applying "The Seven Rs of Selling," and he knows he wants to build **R**apport as well as discover **R**easons to make the **R**ecommendation that will move his sales process forward. In addition, his questions are helping him gain the knowledge he will need to best explain and describe the **R**ewards this customer will receive for following his **R**ecommendations. Tony is intentionally asking well-designed questions to proactively build **R**apport and discover **R**easons for his intended **R**ecommendation.

- **R**esearch forwards the sales strategy and process
- **R**esearch helps us build **R**apport
- **R**esearch discovers **R**easons to make **R**ecommendations
- **R**esearch gathers the knowledge we use to explain and describe **R**ewards

Tony knows that he wants to relate to Mark on a human level. Tony believes that connecting to his clients in some personal way helps them understand how much he cares about them, as well as the work he does for them. Tony is actively searching in every moment for the opportunity to make this connection. When Mark brought up the invisible fence and the dogs, Tony seized this opportunity and in real-time structured his next question, "What kind of dogs do you have?" When Tony asked this question, he already knew he would tell Mark about his childhood dog, Grunter. Mark sharing that he had labs was just an added bonus that made the connection that much better.

In addition to wanting to build **R**apport, Tony also wants to discover **R**easons to make a **R**ecommendation. Tony knows from past experiences that meeting his prospective customers in person leads to more sales. Tony decided a while ago that every time he received an inquiry by phone, he would always recommend a face-to-face meeting rather than try to sell his services on the phone. When Mark said the words, "…I was referred to your company by my neighbor, Sam," Tony already knew that he would recommend a face-to-face meeting in order to forward his sales process. What Tony did not have at that moment were the **R**easons for his **R**ecommendation. By asking, "…can you tell me what you're not happy with right now?" Tony knew that the customer would express his concerns. These concerns became the **R**easons for Tony's intended **R**ecommendation and also provided Tony with the knowledge he needed to explain and describe what Mark would get out of meeting with him.

To fully understand the impact of **R**esearch, let's imagine what Tony's conversation would have been like if he'd tried to make a **R**ecommendation without it:

"Hello, this is Tony."

"Hi Tony, my name is Mark and I was referred to your company by my neighbor, Sam."

"Hi Mark, thanks for calling."

"Sure. Well, we moved here in June and have been using the same company to maintain our lawn as the prior owners, but we're just not happy with them. I just called to see what you would charge us for our yard."

"OK, I'd suggest we meet in person so we can talk about our full range of services."

"Why do we need to do that? Can't you just tell me what you charge?"

Without **Research**, we have no knowledge of the customer and no basis to build **Rapport** or establish trust. We fail to discover **Reasons** to make the **Recommendations** that move the sales process forward. Without **Research**, we are unable to explain and describe the **Rewards**. If we don't discover anything about the customer on a personal level, we have no opening to share anything personal about ourselves. Without personal sharing, we have no basis for a **Relationship**. In summary, without **Research**, we have no **Rapport**, no **Reasons**, no **Rewards**, unfounded **Recommendations**, a poor **Relationship**, a stalled sales process, and poor **Results**.

Fans of the "Trial Close" technique during sales situations will also recognize that **Research** is the key to making this happen. Questions throughout the sales process that confirm the customer's interest in, and desire for, specific products, services, features, options, and details are used to test the customer's commitment. Within the R7 Strategy, every one of these confirmed interests and desires becomes a **Reason** or **Reward** when we make our **Recommendation**. Imagine this conversation:

"Do you like the features of this phone?"

"I love it, it's so easy to use."

Later in the conversation, the practitioner of R7 would say something like, "Well, because you like the feature set and it's so easy to use, I recommend going with this particular phone. It's a great choice, and I know you'll love it!"

We will be exploring **Research** in much more detail in Part Two of this book (Chapter 10). For now, let's move on to **Rapport**.

RAPPORT

The second "R," **Rapport** is essential to connecting with our clients and building trust. Most of us have heard the phrase, "people buy from people they like." Before you discount that phrase, please know directly from my heart, it's true! Giving customers good **Reasons** to support my **Recommendations** is a good strategy. If I do this after I've built trust and

Rapport with my customer, and I've really driven home the point with them that I am on their side, I am unstoppable! When a customer likes me, and trusts me, I am one of the strongest **R**easons for the customer to follow my **R**ecommendations.

One of the biggest barriers for sales professionals to overcome is the stigma and stereotype associated with "salespeople." Years ago, I was involved in a focus group with about 20 customers of a specific brand. In order to spark a transparent conversation, we passed out sheets of blank white paper and boxes of crayons. We asked each of the individuals in the group to draw a picture of a salesperson. The results may, or may not, surprise you. What they drew were mostly animals. Lots of teeth and claws, and mostly predators of some kind; sharks, snakes, rats, badgers, etc. While debriefing with our team we were concerned, but I saw this as a massive opportunity.

I realized that the expectations customers have of salespeople is extremely low. The "bar" is practically lying on the floor and the only thing we have to do to "step over the bar," is be ourselves. The beautiful truth is the vast majority of sales professionals are not sharks, snakes, rats, and badgers. They are genuine, caring, wonderful, and helpful human beings. Salespeople are likable people. Once a customer realizes that you are a decent human being, they don't say to themselves, "Wow, I was wrong about all of the salespeople in the world." Instead, they think, "Wow, with all the sharks, snakes and rats out there, I actually found a decent human being." And now, all they want to do is hold on to you and work with you instead of being, "thrown to the lions."

Let's see how this comes together through the eyes (and ears) of Claire:

Claire the furniture salesperson

Claire is a sales representative for a national high-end furniture store. She's somewhat new to the business and is still getting her bearings. In the last month, she's really hit her stride, and she's looking forward to seeing her commission on her next paycheck. Claire was fifth in the region last month, and she's starting to think she could climb all the way to number one.

Claire has a design background and this is where she shines. She's doing well with multi-room sales and, because of her background, she's able to help her clients with accessories and add-ons. Where she's struggling is on the extended warranty coverage. Claire brings it up with every customer, but she suspects that she could do much better. Claire is contemplating all of this when she overhears a conversation between one of the other consultants and her customer.

> *"This is a beautiful sectional. With the side chair you picked out, will there be seating enough for your whole family?"*
>
> *"I think so, it's just my husband and me, and our two girls."*
>
> *"I've got three at home myself, two boys and a girl."*
>
> *"What's your girl's name? Ours are Amanda and Ellise."*
>
> *"My little girl is Kate and my boys are Jake and Brian…"*

Claire keeps walking as she thinks to herself, *"If I had a dollar for every time I've heard her say, "I've got three at home myself, two boys and a girl." I could retire. Stacy is a little quirky that way, always talking about all her personal stuff with customers."* Stacy is third in the region, and the top performer at this store. Stacy's warranty sales are the highest in the store. *"I wonder how she's pulling that off,"* Claire thinks to herself as she prepares for an appointment with a customer.

A little later, while Claire is working with her customer, she hears Stacy with the same customer as earlier:

"You should definitely get the warranty coverage on this set. With two kids and a dog, too, it's not a question of if you'll need it, but when. I just want you to have peace of mind knowing it's covered."

"Thanks, Stacy, that sounds like good advice."

"You're welcome, it's certainly what I would do if I were making the investment you are. Let me get everything written up and we'll get you on your way."

"OK, thanks."

"That's it?" thinks Claire, "you just tell them to do it, and they do it? That's just too easy!" A few minutes later, Claire decides to try this same method with her customer:

"You should definitely get the warranty coverage on this set, it's not a question of if you'll need it, but when. I don't want you to have to worry about things."

"How much is it?" asks her client, "do you have something that explains the coverage?"

Claire provides the documentation and pricing, but the customer declines the coverage. She decides to embrace a little humility and go have a conversation with Stacy.

"Stacy, do you have a minute?"

"Sure, Claire. What's up?"

"Well, I overheard your conversation earlier and saw how you just told your customer to get the warranty coverage. Do you always cover the warranty that way?"

Stacy thinks about it a moment and then responds, "There's a little bit more to it than that, I think, but in the end, yeah. I pretty much suggest that everyone should do it. There's always a good reason for it."

"I tried it with my customer, and it didn't work at all."

"I think the reason they don't question it is because they know I'm on their side."

Claire asks, "What do you mean?"

"Well, by the time we get to that point, they know me, and they know I care about them. I think they understand that I'm only telling them to get the warranty because I believe it's good for them. I guess they trust me."

"Is that why you're always talking to them about personal stuff?"

Laughing, Stacy replies, "I've just learned to share with them when they share with me."

"But why are all your customers sharing this stuff with you? My customers don't really do that."

"It's not an accident. I ask them questions about their home situation and family intentionally," says Stacy, laughing again.

"Why?"

"So I can share my "personal stuff" with them and help them get to know me a little."

Claire, digesting that comment for a second, says, "I think I'm starting to see the pattern, but I've got a small problem."

"What's that?" asks Stacy.

Claire looks at Stacy and smiles, "I don't have any children."

Stacy chuckles at this, "That's ok, you don't have to be like them, you just have to relate to them. If they don't get to know you a little, how can they trust your advice? If they tell you about their children, just tell them that you don't have any…yet."

"Hey now, let's not get ahead of ourselves," says Claire, laughing now. "Thanks for the advice."

Claire thinks she's starting to understand the value of getting to know her customers a little better, but she's wondering what she's going to tell them about herself. Let's explore this a little further.

Building **R**apport is not just finding out about your customers and their lives, it is also allowing your customers to find out a little about you. **R**apport is discovering a bit of your customer's truth and connecting that truth to your own in some way. One of the best ways to grasp this concept is to understand both what **R**apport is, and what it is not:

What Rapport is

- **R**apport is connecting and relating.
    - **R**apport is about sharing the human condition with another person. This is your chance to prove to them that you are not a shark, snake, rat or badger. Step over the bar!
- **R**apport is genuine, real, human and true.
    - **R**apport is about being your true self. What about you is memorable and relatable? There is no need to exaggerate or lie. Don't embellish things, just be yourself!
- **R**apport is simple and brief.
    - **R**apport is intertwined in your conversations with your customers as small "snippets" of information shared between you, for example, "I've got three at home myself, two boys and a girl." This conversation doesn't need to go any further unless the customer chooses to. Share something memorable and move on!
- **R**apport is intentional.
    - While the best salespeople I've met are fantastic at building rapport naturally, no salespeople I've met do it every time unless they do it intentionally. As much as you might believe it's something that "just happens," believe me when I tell you it doesn't. **R**apport does not happen consistently by accident. All you have to do to see this in play is ask yourself, "What does my customer know about me? If the answer is, "nothing," which it often is, this is a clear indication that you need to incorporate it more intentionally. This is how **R**esearch connects to **R**apport. Ask a question to allow your customer to share something, and then relate to what they've told you. Do not leave **R**apport up to

chance, do it on purpose.

What Rapport is not

- **R**apport is not an interview or an interrogation.
  - **R**apport is not a list of questions you ask your customer to dissect their lives until you find something in common. "Do you have kids?… What are their names?…How old are they?…What sports do they play?" Don't interrogate them!
- **R**apport is not uncomfortable or awkward.
  - **R**apport must flow in the context of your conversation. Above, Stacy asked, "…will there be seating enough for your whole family?" which fits the conversation. Imagine how awkward it could have been otherwise. "This is a beautiful sectional. Do you have kids?" Additionally, if the customer doesn't engage in a personal way, don't keep trying. If the customer had responded with a simple, "Yes," to the question, "…will there be seating enough for the whole family?" it would have been awkward for Stacy to ask more questions about anything personal at that point. Don't force it!
- **R**apport is not "being the same."
  - **R**apport is not, "Me, too!" While many people think rapport is built by finding commonalities, I believe rapport is created by simply connecting and relating on a human level. This should be one of the most enjoyable parts of your job. You don't have to try to find something that is the same. Share your truth!
- **R**apport is not about "over sharing" and it's not all about you.
  - **R**apport is not all about you, but it is about how you relate to them. Imagine this dialogue, "…it's just my husband and I and our two girls," says the customer. "I grew up in San Francisco," says Stacy. What? And that matters, why? This is both awkward and completely unrelated. Focus on what they are sharing rather than what you want to share. Also, this is not an opportunity for you to brag or tell stories and monopolize the customer's time. If you've done this intentionally, then you have influenced the topic of the conversation, which should allow you to share something that you enjoy sharing. Celebrate your customer, don't "one up"

them or over share. "This one time, at band camp…" should not be in your sales vocabulary. Don't make it about you.

- **R**apport is not an act.
  - The digital world provides ample opportunity for consumers to make purchases without dealing with another human being. The fact that they've chosen to do so is revealing and important. If you are in a sales or advisory profession today, connecting with other people and caring about them should be something you enjoy doing. If you have to act like you care, you are likely in the wrong profession. I once had a sales manager ask me, "How do I get my people to act like they care?" Can you guess what my response might have been?

Claire the furniture salesperson, continued

Luckily, Claire set up an appointment today with a customer she spoke with on the phone yesterday. Let's take a look at how Claire might use these techniques during her appointment:

"Welcome, Mrs. Stevenson, thanks for coming in today."

"Hi Claire, just call me Brenda. Thanks for setting this up."

"You're welcome. I understand you're looking to refresh your family room, is this a complete refresh or are we replacing just a piece or two?"

"No, we have a blank slate, the room is pretty much empty right now."

"OK Brenda, have you been in the home a while?"

"No, actually we moved from Denver just a month ago."

"Oh," says Claire, "I've never been to Denver, what brought you here?"

"My husband's company offered us a relocation and we always wanted to come here," Brenda replied, *"It happened pretty fast, and here we are."*

"I've lived here my whole life," says Claire, *"so if you need some ideas for good restaurants or anything, just ask. Let's take a look at some*

options and maximize your time. I'm sure you're going to love it here, but moving is hectic. I bet you still have boxes to unpack."

"Yes, we do. I try to tackle a couple more each day. I'd love to know where the good restaurants are, we really haven't been out and about much yet..."

Claire is feeling pretty good about her conversation. She is well on her way toward establishing **R**apport and connecting with her client. Let's take a closer look at this conversation:

- The conversation lasted approximately 45 seconds
- Claire conducted **R**esearch. She asked three questions.
- The customer knows that Claire has never been to Denver, and that she has lived "here" her whole life. The customer also perceives that Claire understands her current situation and wants to be helpful.
- Claire knows that Brenda and her family have just moved from Denver due to her husband's job relocation, which happened quite quickly. She also knows they are still doing some unpacking and they haven't "been out and about much yet."
- Claire is successfully building **R**apport.
- There are several **R**easons for Brenda to move forward in the process, chief among them is maximizing her time.
- Claire is advancing the process forward with, "Let's take a look at some options and maximize your time…" which is a **R**ecommendation followed by a **R**eward.
- As they continue their conversation about furnishing Brenda's family room, it is likely they will talk about the area and local restaurants. Claire is being helpful on multiple levels. This is the beginning of a **R**elationship.
- When Claire recommends that Brenda include the protection plan with her new furniture, do you think she'll get a good response? I do. **R**esults!

When you are successful at building **R**apport, you will have more involved and productive conversations with your customers. In this way,

Rapport actually enhances your **Research**. Conversely, it is your initial **Research** that leads to finding a "sharing moment" with your customer. **Research** leads to **Rapport** and **Rapport** enhances **Research**. Once you've established a connection of some kind and related to your customer, you've bolstered your credibility and strengthened your position as a guide, advisor and consultant.

REASONS, RECOMMENDATIONS & REWARDS

In addition to opening the door to building **Rapport**, one of the primary purposes of **Research** is to discover **Reasons**. As you've learned previously, the primary purpose of an advisor, consultant and guide is to make **Recommendations**. **Reasons** are the basis for all **Recommendations** and all **Recommendations** should be followed by **Rewards**. While **Reasons** provide the logical rationale for a customer to move forward, **Rewards** supply the emotional motivation. The combination of **Reasons**, **Recommendations**, and **Rewards** is a, "Recommendation Statement." Let me see if I can clean this up for you:

- One of the primary purposes of **Research** is to discover **Reasons**.
- **Reasons** are the basis for all **Recommendations**.
- **Recommendations** should always be followed by **Rewards**.
- **Reasons** and **Rewards** provide the logical rationale and the emotional motivation to move forward in the sales process - which leads to **Results**.

Because **Reasons**, **Recommendations** and **Rewards** are so closely tied together, it is extremely difficult to discuss one without the other. For the purpose of giving you a clear understanding, I will cover them together in this section.

Before I go too much further, I want to cover a key point with regard to **Recommendations**. While I use this particular word within the R7 Strategy, in practical use and everyday language, we do not always use the word, "recommend." There are many ways for a consulting professional to recommend a product, service or course of action without saying, "I recommend." In particular, you will want to moderate your language based on your perceived level of expertise and credibility. Sometimes you will want to take a more prescriptive approach with a strong **R**ecommendation, and other times you will want to soften your advice with a gentle suggestion. In general, the more credibility and trust you have, the more direct you may be with your approach.

In addition, if you are recommending a service-based solution or course of action, you may want to involve your customer in the decision to create more long-term commitment to the solution. In order to do that, you will use gentle leading language and allow them to make a decision. This gives them ownership of the solution. Here are a few examples of **R**ecommendations phrased in different ways:

- "You might consider opening both the checking and savings account today…"
- "Many of my customers find it very helpful to…"
- "The most common approach is to…"
- "This is the highest rated brand, so I'd suggest…"
- "The logical next step for you would be to…."
- "If it were me, I would…"
- "You should really consider…"
- "The best course of action is…"
- "Let's finalize the color choices and then move on to…"

As you can see, there are endless ways to lead into this element of R7. For simplification throughout the rest of this chapter, I will use, "I **R**ecommend." It's worth noting that there are multiple ways to lead into the **R**easons and **R**ewards as well. I will provide quite a few different examples in Chapter 12 when we revisit this topic.

It's essential to understand that **R**ecommendations are at the very core of R7. It's not a coincidence that it sits right in the middle of the Seven Rs. It's worth repeating; within the R7 strategy, everything either leads up to, or flows from, the **R**ecommendation. Let's see how this comes together in the next example:

Steve the automotive salesperson

Steve is a veteran salesperson with more than 20 years of experience in multiple automotive brands. He's been with his current dealership for 12 years, and he is one of the most consistent salespeople at the dealership, selling an average of 16 cars per month. Even though he's been consistent, his income has been decreasing due to shrinking margins. About a third of his sales every month are from previous customers, but two thirds of his customers are new. He's scanning his inbox when the phone rings:

"Thank you for holding, this is Steve, how can I help you today?"

"Hello, I was looking at your website and I found a silver SUV I'm interested in. I just want to know if it's still available and get some pricing information."

"Sure. Again, I'm Steve, may I know who I'm speaking with?"

"My name's Jess."

"Hi Jess, I'll take a look for you. Did you happen to get the VIN number from our website?"

"I did actually," says Jess, giving Steve the VIN.

Here there's a pause of 30 seconds while Steve looks up the vehicle.

"Good news, Jess, that vehicle is still available, when would you like to come in and take it for a drive?"

"Right now, I'm just trying to find out what my payment would be on a lease. I'm making a few calls to see who can give me the lowest payment."

"Ok, give me a minute."

Another pause, this time for just under a minute.

"Jess?"

"Yeah, I'm still here."

"So, it looks like we can get your payment down to around $395 per month. Do you want to set up a time to come and take a look at the car?"

"Not right now. Thanks for your help, Steve. Let me go over all the information I've been collecting and I'll call you back."

"Sure, my direct line is…."

Let's do a little analysis:

- This conversation lasted two and a half minutes, during which Jess was on hold 90 seconds (half of the call).
- Steve asked exactly three questions (**R**esearch). "How can I help you today?" "When would you like to come in and take it for a drive?" and, "Do you want to set up a time to come and take a look at the car?"
- Steve knows almost nothing about the customer. The customer knows almost nothing about Steve. No **R**apport.
- Steve made no **R**ecommendations. He *asked* Jess if she wanted to come in, but he didn't *recommend* that she do so. There is a huge difference, as I will explain below.
- Steve gave no **R**easons and provided no **R**ewards for Jess to take the next step.

To understand the interplay between **R**easons, **R**ecommendations and **R**ewards, we first need to understand the difference between a **R**ecommendation by a consultant, and a question from a customer service agent. A customer service professional asks questions that have no consequences. There are no repercussions involved in the choice. Here are some examples:

- "Would you like cream or sugar with your coffee?"
- "Would you prefer an aisle or a window seat?"
- "What flavor would you like?"
- "Do you want to stay on a higher or a lower floor?"

There is a big difference between *asking* and *recommending*. Can you imagine a waiter saying, "I highly recommend cream and sugar with your coffee?" Just as that seems a bit funny to think about, it would be just as ridiculous for a consultant to ask a question, rather than make a **R**ecommendation. Consider these examples:

- "Do you want to go with a guilty plea, or try an insanity defense?"
- "What type of psychotherapy do you want?"
- "How would you like me to build the foundation of your new home?"
- "How do you want to configure your investments to maximize your return?"

In all of these examples, our response would likely be, "I don't know! What would you **RECOMMEND**?" When there are consequences to our choices and someone is supposed to be guiding us, we expect them to provide advice and direction. Unfortunately, the **R**ecommendation is not enough by itself. Let's rephrase the above examples into advice and guidance, instead of questions:

- "I recommend you plead guilty."
- "I recommend group therapy."
- "I recommend a solid concrete foundation."
- "I recommend 40% bonds and 60% equities for your investment portfolio."

In every one of these cases, it is extremely likely that we would ask, "Why?" What are the **R**easons for this **R**ecommendation? A good consultant provides the **R**easons along with the **R**ecommendation to answer these questions proactively. This provides the individual with the rationale needed to make a decision. **R**easons answer the question, "Does it make sense to follow this **R**ecommendation?" Once the reasons have been shared and the **R**ecommendation given, **R**ewards should follow. The **R**ewards answer the questions, "Do I *want* to follow that **R**ecommendation?" and, "Am I motivated to follow that **R**ecommendation?" While **R**easons are logical, **R**ewards are emotional. When the **R**easons are valid and the **R**ewards are clear, it is very difficult not to follow the **R**ecommendation. While good consultants always provide **R**easons and **R**ecommendations together, only the best blend **R**easons, **R**ecommendations and **R**ewards. Just follow the formula; **R**easons - **R**ecommendation - **R**ewards.

Let's take a look at a well-known consultative and helping profession, medicine. Have a look at these three **R**ecommendations:

- "I recommend you have surgery right away."
- "Because this condition could get worse, I recommend surgery right away."
- "Because this condition could get worse, I recommend surgery right away so you won't have to worry about it getting worse. I want you to begin the recovery process so you can get back to being healthy."

Which of these three is the strongest message? Which is the most persuasive, influential and compelling? If we, as salespeople are truly advocating for our customer's benefit, it matters to us that they do what we are suggesting. There are negative consequences when the customer doesn't follow our advice.

It is also important to understand that, in an ongoing sales conversation or consultation with a client, it is extremely rare to make only one **R**ecommendation. It is very common to give advice and guidance multiple times. Do you recall Tony the landscaper from the beginning of this chapter? He **R**ecommended a face-to-face meeting with Mark. During that meeting, he will likely **R**ecommend a frequency of maintenance visits, particular plants to use for landscaping, etc. For each **R**ecommendation, he should follow the steps of R7 and make a "**R**ecommendation Statement" using the **R**eason-**R**ecommendation-**R**eward formula. At some point toward the end of the consultation, he'll **R**ecommend getting a signed contract in place so they can schedule their first lawn maintenance visit, and voila!

As we shall see in future chapters, the sales process helps define the steps we want to take with our customer. These steps frame the **R**ecommendations we will make. In other words, if I know what the next steps of the process are, then I know what **R**ecommendations I will be making. With that in mind I only need to discover the **R**easons to go there. When we conduct our **R**esearch by asking questions, we are discovering **R**easons to move forward through the sales process. **R**easons answer these questions:

- Why this product, service or course of action?
- Why this particular next step?
- Why now?
- Why do this with my organization?
- Why do this with me?

Steve the automotive salesperson, continued

Let's see how Steve might have used this with Jess:

"Thank you for holding, this is Steve, how can I help you today?"

"Hello, I was looking at your website and I found a silver SUV I'm interested in. I just want to know if it's still available and get some pricing information."

"Sure. Again, I'm Steve, may I know who I'm speaking with?"

"My name's Jess."

"Hi Jess, I'll take a look for you. Have you owned this brand before?"

"No, this would be my first."

"Wonderful, I'm sure you'll love it. My wife drives the model just a bit smaller than this one, but we just became empty-nesters so she doesn't really need the bigger one anymore."

"We've still got a ways to go; ours are only eight and 10."

"It goes fast, so enjoy it. It feels like mine were that age just yesterday. Listen, I see we actually have several of them in silver, have you seen this color in person yet?"

"Only on the internet," says Jess, "I really like it."

"It's really a beautiful car," replies Steve, "Are you looking at doing something soon or do I have some time to work on this for you?"

"My current lease is up in about a month so I'm hoping to do something by then."

"Ok, Jess. Since your lease is up in just a month and you really haven't seen this car in person yet, I'd recommend that we set up a time for you to see the car and drive it. I can give you a proper introduction to the brand and go over all the options with you. We can get everything ironed out so you don't have to worry about your lease coming to an end soon..."

Let's compare this to the previous conversation:

- This conversation lasted only two minutes, which is 30 seconds less than the previous conversation.
- Steve asked five questions (**R**esearch), including, "have you owned this brand before?" "have you seen this color in person?" and, "are you looking at doing something soon, or do I have some time to work on this for you?"
- Steve knows that Jess has two children, eight and 10. He also knows that she is new to the brand, has not seen the car in person, and is 30 days away from the end of her current lease. (All **R**easons for his intended **R**ecommendation)
- The customer knows that Steve is married, his wife drives a similar car, and they recently became empty nesters. He is well on his way to building **R**apport.
- Steve provided excellent **R**easons for his strong **R**ecommendation and followed his **R**ecommendation with **R**ewards.
- There were no uncomfortable pauses in the conversation because Steve filled the time with conversation.

This scenario is also much better for Jess. In the first scenario, she received a lease payment that may or may not be valid for what she intends to purchase and is probably not comparable with other numbers she's been getting from other dealers. To calculate a lease payment, here are some of the variables:

- The purchase price of the vehicle.
- The amount of the "down payment" or security deposit.

- Jess' creditworthiness via her credit "score."
- The region/state where the vehicle will be registered (tax rate variations).
- The number of miles per year the vehicle will be driven (10,000, 12,000, 15,000).
- The term of the lease (three years, four years, etc.).
- Equity (or negative equity) in her current vehicle based on value and condition.

When she was quoted a lease payment of $395, was it a three, four, or five year term? Was it for 10,000, 12,000, or 15,000 miles per year? What region/state were the taxes calculated for? Were taxes included at all? If she's comparing Steve's payment of $395 to another dealer's quoted payment of $375, which one is better? We can't answer that question due to all the variables. Are the two vehicles being compared equipped exactly the same way? Are both quotes for the same down payment, same tax rate, same miles per year and same lease term? It's likely that they are not. When you add the knowledge that Jess hasn't seen this color in person, is new to the brand and only has 30 days left on her lease, it becomes clear that her best course of action is to sit down with someone she trusts, resolve all the variables above and make the choices that are best for her and her family. Of course, this is *exactly* what Steve **R**ecommended. Well done!

I started this section by explaining how **R**easons, **R**ecommendations and **R**ewards are always intertwined. Whenever we are attempting to advise and guide our customers, we should explain to them what we believe they should do, why we believe they should do it, and what we believe they will get out of it. Let's move on to R6, **R**elationship.

RELATIONSHIP

Do you like people? I sincerely hope you answered with a resounding, "Yes." In fact, for the purposes of this section, I'm going to assume that you did. I'm not going to ask if you didn't…you did, right? Most of the successful sales professionals I've worked with agree: the relationship we build with our customers is the most rewarding part of the job. I've spent a long time in the profession of sales, and I can honestly say that quite a few of my clients have become some of my best friends, mentors and promoters. My clients challenge me, inspire me and give me my professional purpose. Because of them, I have a professional sense of fulfillment.

Getting to know and be involved with new people is the most exciting part of what I do for a living. When we graduate from "selling stuff," to "helping people," our career in sales transforms into problem-solving, improving situations and celebrating life. This requires us to become an advocate for our customer. While **R**apport is a human connection that can be established quite quickly, the **R**elationship is earned over time. **R**apport establishes your humanity, but the **R**elationship proves over time that you care more about your customer's well-being than you do about one transaction.

What must we do over time to build positive **R**elationships? Here are a few of my thoughts:

Be fair and transparent. I don't have to tell you what "fair" is in your industry or position. You already know. If you feel you've delivered a fair value for what you're asking and your customer is happy with the end result, then you are in the right place. From a transparency perspective, just be honest and open with your customers. This does not mean that customers have a right to audit our books or see the inner workings of what we do. Being transparent might include informing a customer that you don't share that information. Don't try to trick them or delude them, just help them understand the truth. If you are being fair, this should be an easy thing to do.

There is also a tremendous benefit to timing and choreographing the disclosure of information. What does the customer need to know at the different stages of the process to make the best decision? Usually it's best for both the salesperson and the customer to fully understand the product or service offering and the different variables involved before a final price is presented. Price is rarely the best data point to base a decision on. In the prior section, had Jess made a decision based on the $375 payment offered by another dealership, everything might have gone downhill from there. How would she react when all the variables came to light, and her monthly payment jumped to $445.

Think long-term! Make your decisions and take care of your customers with a long-term view. This may not gain you the "big sale," in the near term, but it will pay off down the road through your positive **R**elationships and outstanding reputation. There have been plenty of times in my career when short-term gains have been sacrificed for a long-term **R**elationship. There have been times for me personally where I made the wrong decision in this regard as well - and I have regretted every one of them. It's not always easy to do the right thing, but it's still the right thing to do.

Be yourself and enjoy yourself. All of the best sales professionals that I've worked with over the years have this quality in common. They are fun to be around, mostly because of their vulnerability and willingness to just be themselves. We all know someone in our work environments who never lets their guard down, and walks around with a somewhat manufactured persona. I don't know about you, but this is always uncomfortable for me. I find myself thinking, *"I wonder who they really are on the inside,"* and it creates a barrier between us. Conversely, it's also not a good idea to disregard your social filter and engage customers with inappropriate, reckless abandon either.

RESULTS

Results come from practicing and repeating the R7 methodology consistently. **R**esults are present in the pride you feel when you've acted in the best interests of your customer and your organization simultaneously. **R**esults exist in the knowledge that you've grown and adapted to new circumstances. **R**esults come from high customer satisfaction and positive feedback. **R**esults are what you feel when you realize you are at the top of your game and loving every minute of it.

As you begin incorporating these strategies into your daily conversation and communication, you will soon realize that these strategies will become a part of the way you communicate in any "helping relationship." You will come to see that, whether you are acting as a sales professional, parent, teacher, friend or concerned citizen, R7 will give you the framework you need to be more influential and persuasive and therefore, more helpful.

To achieve a highly successful career in sales, you will first have to define what success looks like for you. Success has a different meaning for everyone. For some, it's having a comfortable, steady income. For some, it's being number one in their region, division, company or industry. How will you know when you've achieved this goal? Only you can decide what this is for you. Once you've decided, break it down into pieces. Set near-term and intermediate goals in line with your ultimate definition of success and then pursue these goals diligently and relentlessly.

In order to define your goals and measure success, go backwards through your sales process. Let's look at an example:

Brian the software salesperson

Brian has been working as a sales advisor for an online software company. They sell software as a service via a subscription model. Last year, he was third in his company. This year, his goal is to be number one. He knows who his competitors are and what they've been selling and he's calculated the number he'll have to achieve. His goal is to sell 700 subscriptions this year. At first, this seemed like an unachievable goal, but as he started to break it down, it became much more realistic. The first thing he did was reduce it to a monthly goal of 60 subscriptions.

Brian looked at his sales process and began breaking it down into pieces. He also analyzed his past sales numbers and activities in order to understand where he needed to improve. Ultimately, this is what his monthly goal sheet looked like:

Monthly Goals:

Outbound Email Responses:	800
Initial Phone Conversations:	200 (25%)
Software Demos:	120 (60%)
30 Day Trials:	90 (75%)
Sales	60 (66%)

By reversing his sales process and looking from the end result backwards, he realizes that he needs to sell 90 "30 day trials" each month to close 60 sales. This is based on his current closing ratio from trials to subscriptions, which is two out of three (66%). He then looks backward one more step. To get 90 "30 day trials," he will need to conduct 120 software demonstrations. Using this same method, he realizes he needs to have 200 monthly phone conversations and he will need to send out 800 customized email responses each month. Looking back at all of this, Brian realizes that if he can maintain his current success rates through the process, all he has to do is increase the number of outbound emails he is sending every day to 40. Statistically, this will result in 10 phone calls a day with new potential customers and six scheduled demos every day.

Daily Goals:

Outbound email Responses:	40
Initial Phone Conversations:	10 (25%)
Software Demos:	6 (60%)
30 Day Trials:	4.5 (75%)
Sales:	3 (66%)

Brian next reviews the overall effort to see what the time commitment would be. The software demos take approximately 20 minutes each; allowing for time in between to setup, this effort is about three hours each day. Another 90 minutes allowed for phone conversations and a further 90 minutes for sending custom emails, and he's up to six hours. This allows him time to follow up on all of his 30 day trials to gain the final commitment and complete all of his CRM and administrative tasks. His days are going to be busy, but his plan is definitely doable.

Lastly, Brian should look at each step of his process to see if there is an opportunity to improve his ratios between steps. This is the quality element of his efforts. Rather than simply do more, more, more, he could practice new strategies and techniques in order to achieve more with a higher quality effort. I will discuss the aspects of quality and quantity when I revisit **R**esults in Chapter 14.

R7: PUTTING IT ALL TOGETHER

In Part Three of this book (Chapters 10 to 14) I provide more examples, as well as a deeper understanding of *how* to incorporate these strategies. For now, let's review some of the key elements of R7. When you are interacting in real-time with your customer, you will rely on R1 to R5. For some, it helps to think of this process as "discovery and direction." When we are asking questions and gaining understanding we are discovering and when we are giving advice we are directing. It might help to review the R7 graphic at the beginning of this chapter. It is quite common in most sales scenarios to cycle through the first five Rs multiple times before completing a transaction, (and moving on to **Relationship** and **Results**).

Research

Research is intentional. It's not about satisfying your curiosity. **Research** positions you as the leader in a consultative situation. The person asking the questions is the leader. These questions are not random. Your questions should be strategic, opening the door to building **R**apport and discovering **R**easons to move forward with a **R**ecommendation. Be intentional. Ask the right questions in the right way. **R**esearch leads to **R**easons and **R**apport.

Rapport

Rapport is a connection between two people, which can be established fairly quickly through a process of sharing. Use **R**esearch to ask situationally relevant questions to encourage your customer to share with you, and then *relate* to what they have shared. In my experience, this happens naturally for the best of us about 30 percent of the time. You must be intentional about building **R**apport. Customers' expectations of sales professionals are fairly low. Use this as an opportunity to "step over the bar." **R**apport helps to establish trust and create a comfortable, stress-free working relationship. It is *not* about being the same. Don't be, "me too," just be yourself. Connect your truth to your customer's truth.

Reasons

Reasons are the basis for your **R**ecommendations. **R**easons help you proactively answer the question, "Why?" We use **R**esearch to fully understand and "diagnose" the customer's situation before we give advice. Using this method, our advice and guidance are always valid and based on the **R**easons the customer provided. At times, the information you discover leads to your **R**ecommendation. Other times, you have a **R**ecommendation you would like to make, and you need to discover the **R**easons to do so. Good **R**easons reduce the customer's sense of risk.

Recommendations

In a consultative conversation, everything leads up to, or flows from, the **R**ecommendation. Stop asking your customers if they want to move forward; **R**ecommend it instead. At any given time in the sales process, there is a "next step." This step should be the focus of your **R**ecommendation. There are consequences for the customer if they do not follow your **R**ecommendation; there is something they are not going to get, something they will not be able to do, something that will not happen as a result. Make your **R**ecommendations with passion, conviction and confidence.

Rewards

Rewards provide the emotional motivation to move forward. By describing the **R**ewards, you are individualizing and tailoring your message as well as proactively answering the question, "What's in it for me?" When you follow **R**ecommendations with unique **R**ewards, the customer recognizes you listened to them, and you have a more thorough understanding of what they are trying to accomplish. After hearing the **R**ewards you have described, your customer should say, "I really want this! This is going to be great for me."

Relationship

Rapport can be established fairly quickly. A **R**elationship is earned over time. The keys to a positive **R**elationship are transparency, consistency and caring. When your customer perceives that you care about them, their sense of loyalty toward you grows. If you show them consistency in your personal attention and professional ability, they will come to depend on you. Positive **R**elationships with your customers will be the key to a long-term, successful career. These **R**elationships are the absolute best source of repeat and referral business.

Results

Learning, practicing and using the R7 strategy will lead to more satisfied customers and a greater sense of accomplishment. You will be more influential and persuasive in all interactions (not just those involving a customer.) You will graduate from "selling stuff," to "helping people." In the process of doing so, you will be more successful and rewarded. You will learn to measure and track all the stages of your sales process as an avenue toward future personal growth. Based on your **R**esults you will know where to focus your individual improvement efforts.

Summary

The R7 strategy is not always linear, and almost never happens only once in a conversation with a customer. The elements of R7 are repeated over and over again as you move freely between discovery, direction and development. **R**apport is not something you do at a particular point in time during the sales process. Instead, it is a continuous part of the process. I've presented R7 here linearly for the purposes of easy understanding but, as you practice it, you will want to embrace flexibility.

Key Takeaways – Chapter Four

- The key to consultative sales is having an intentional approach to discovering needs and providing advice.
- **R**esearch is the key to leading the conversation and discovering deeper needs.
- Everything flows to or from the **R**ecommendation.
- The **R**elationship is essential to long-term success and individual fulfillment.

CHAPTER FIVE
STEP FORWARD

"When we are 'in the moment' with our customer, every piece of information we provide, every question we ask, and every move we make influences the next steps in the process as well as the overall outcome."

STEP FORWARD

S | **STRATEGIC**
Move through the process intentionally.
Micro steps lead to macro steps. Think ahead.

T | **TIMELY**
Take each step when the time is right. Too
early is aggressive, too late is inefficient.

E | **EXPLICIT**
Share your process with your customer.
Explain what you're doing and why.

P | **PURPOSEFUL**
Satisfy both function and purpose. Your
customer should enjoy your process.

OUTCOME ORIENTATION

Now that you've had an introduction to *The Seven Rs of Selling*, I want to discuss how we use a consultative methodology to move through the sales process. One of the most important qualities of a leader is what I call, "Outcome Orientation." Stated plainly, this is the constant awareness of an individual's vision and mission, as well as the very next steps along the path to achieving victory (however victory is defined). As I have stated previously, a consultative sales professional must lead the interactions with prospective customers. When you lead, you are able to choreograph their experience, both chronologically and qualitatively.

The moment we lose sight of where we are going next, the customer may ask a question or pose an objection that will divert us from moving forward in the sales process. When this happens, we become reactive. As we begin reacting, we lose control of the situation, which is detrimental to both parties. In some circumstances, we ask a question or make a comment either in direct opposition to, or completely unrelated to, where we are trying to guide our customer. In effect, we derail our own process.

You must constantly consider both the overall outcome and the **very next steps** to get there. To properly advise and guide your clients, you will need to have a plan. In short, you need to be strategic. Consider the following examples:

Scenario One

"OK, it looks like you've decided on your cooking appliances. Do you have a refrigerator in mind?"

"We were looking for a French door model in stainless, with a water and ice dispenser."

"Great, let me see what I have…"

Scenario Two

"OK, it looks like you've decided on your cooking appliances. Let's take a look at refrigeration needs. You mentioned earlier that you do a lot of cooking at home, do you use a lot of fresh ingredients?"

"Yes, we buy organic most of the time."

"My wife and I try to do the same; it's a bit more costly, but definitely worth it. How often do you typically go grocery shopping?"

"We go about once a week, sometimes twice."

"Based on the size of your family, as well as your cooking and shopping habits, I would suggest we look at some of our larger capacity refrigerators. This way you won't have to change your routine habits in your new kitchen. I have a few I'd like to show you…"

In Scenario One, the sales consultant asked, "Do you have a refrigerator in mind?" The customer's answer to this question immediately and severely limited the available product choices. In addition, we have put the customer in the "lead" role. There are consequences to this course of action. In this scenario, we have a list of customer preferences that may or may not be available, and the preferences stated by the customer may lead to a choice that does not have sufficient capacity. In addition, this is an inefficient way to move through the sales process and will take more time to make final choices. As we learned earlier, when there are consequences involved, we don't ask, we **Recommend**.

In Scenario Two, the sales consultant believes the primary purpose of a refrigerator is food preservation. By understanding the customer's needs and preferences in this area, they were able to move forward efficiently in the sales process with a strong "Recommendation Statement," combining R3, R4, and R5

It is extremely important to understand that a different consultant under different circumstances might have wanted to narrow down design and aesthetic choices prior to moving on to capacity choices, and that is perfectly acceptable! Different organizations follow different processes. Outcome Orientation simply requires that we know where we are going at all times. When the next step in the process is clear to us, we know our next **Recommendation** will be to take that step. This provides the consumer with a professional and efficient process - boosting your credibility and further establishing your role as a consultant, rather than a transactional salesperson.

The sales professional's inner dialogue sounds something like this, *"What's the best 'next step' for my customer? Okay, so that will be my **R**ecommendation. What are good solid **R**easons to make that **R**ecommendation? Do these **R**easons exist for this customer? Hmm. I don't know, let's ask…"* The desired outcome greatly influences the **R**ecommendation you will make. We must have **R**easons to make **R**ecommendations, so based on the intended outcome, we formulate our **R**esearch questions.

STEP FORWARD

Once you decide to make the transition from being reactive to being intentional about leading your client through the sales process, you will quickly realize that it's not as easy as it sounds. In order to help you master this concept, I created the STEP Model. STEP stands for Strategic, Timely, Explicit, and Purposeful. Let me break these down for you:

Strategic

There is a plan! To move forward in the sales process intentionally and efficiently, you will need to be strategic. Just as in most games of strategy, you will have to understand the overall goals and long-term plans, as well as the very next "move." Just as in the game of chess, you must think several moves ahead, make your moves in order, and be able to modify your strategy "on the fly," based on the moves of your opponent. Unlike the game of chess, however, our customer is not an opponent and we are often making moves together to achieve a jointly beneficial outcome. When you execute these moves in succession, you will find you are setting yourself up extremely well for success. When we succeed, both sides win! All of our strategies, plans, goals, and outcomes are in service to our customer.

When we are "in the moment" with our customer, every piece of information we provide, every question we ask, and every move we make influences the next steps in the process as well as the overall outcome. We must be aware of this at all times in order to help the customer to the best of our ability.

Timely

Each move you make must be timely. In my experience, timeliness is most frequently violated when we move too soon. This happens extremely often. Fortunately, it's usually easy to spot. Here are a few examples:

- We give a **R**ecommendation without a **R**eason.
    - Do your **R**esearch to find **R**easons and then make your **R**ecommendation.
- We give a **R**ecommendation with a **R**eason, but the **R**eason was assumed rather than stated by the customer.
    - Even if your assumption is true, your **R**ecommendation will carry more weight if the **R**eason is stated by the customer. Verify your assumption by doing your **R**esearch.
- We give a great Recommendation prior to establishing **R**apport.
    - Your customers will be much more likely to follow your advice if there is an element of trust. Ask questions that allow you to share and establish your humanity.
- We unnecessarily discuss pricing too early in the conversation.
    - When price enters the conversation, the customer begins the decision-making process. If you have not had the chance to build the full value of your offering, it's best to navigate price more delicately, rather than facing it head on.
    - Don't use price to "qualify" your customer and save yourself time. What the customer can afford and is willing to pay will change throughout the process as value is established.
- We skip single or multiple steps in the sales process.
    - This jeopardizes the forward momentum of the sales process, creates discomfort, and often feels awkward to the customer. It also can lead to prematurely discussing price before value is created or understood.

The reverse of moving too soon is moving too late. This often happens when we are "overselling." At each stage in the process, you should constantly be asking yourself, "Has the customer given me good **R**easons to move forward to the next stage in the process? Have I built enough value in my offering to move on? Have I established **R**apport?" If you have established **R**apport, built value, and have the **R**easons you need to move forward, then do so! At this very moment, the customer is most likely to act upon your **R**ecommendation. Be aware that every moment that passes from this point and every word spoken by either party diminishes this likelihood. Consider the following example:

Scenario One

"Are you looking for something you can take home today?"

"Yes, we want to be able to use it this weekend."

"Based on what you've told me, this TV should be a good size for your family room."

"I think so too. I love the picture, and the price is so reasonable!"

"Yes, it's on sale because the newer version is coming out in a month or so."

"Oh? What's different on the newer version?"

"It's a little thinner and it has a few more bells and whistles."

"I don't want to wait a month, but maybe I should look at a thinner model…"

Scenario Two

"Are you looking for something you can take home today?"

"Yes, we want to be able to use it this weekend."

"Based on what you've told me, this TV should be a good size for your family room."

"I think so too. I love the picture, and the price is so reasonable!"

"Sounds like we've selected the right one then, let me set one aside for you while we look at mounting options and cable requirements. Are you planning to mount the TV to the wall?"

"Yes we are. Thank you."

As you can see, there comes a time when the customer is ready to move forward both logically and emotionally. Everything that happens between that moment and moving on jeopardizes the chances of moving forward. Being aware of this moment is a behavioral skill that's developed over time.

In Scenario One, the sales representative attempted to explain why the price was "so reasonable." In my opinion, this is overselling. In Scenario Two, the sales representative recognized that it was time to move forward and did so. The customer needed a TV for the weekend, loved the picture and the price, and was ready to move forward. Newer features a month from now won't be helpful.

Explicit

The steps of the sales process should be explicit. To be open and transparent with our customers, we should tell them what we *are* doing for them as well as what we *will* be doing for them. One of the errors we often make is not setting ourselves up for future steps. If we are thinking and planning ahead, we should be preparing them to move through the process. Explain the process to them so they understand ahead of time what's coming. This way, when we get to that future step, it is logical and flows well. When there are decisions the customer has to make, surprises are often extremely detrimental to a positive outcome. Also, if your intent is to cover price toward the end, explain that to your customer early (and give a reason for doing so). Consider the following example:

"Thank you for considering our services. We want to make sure we customize a solution for you that does exactly what you need it to do. We also want to be able to recommend some things to help future-proof your business and keep your customer data secure. We know that no implementation is exactly the same, so we'll work with your team to clearly understand your situation. Once we have a proposal together for you, we'll cover what we believe the minimum requirements are as well as some options that may be of tremendous benefit. This will also allow us to tailor the pricing to only those services that you will be taking advantage of."

By explaining your process in a way that makes sense for the customer, you earn the right to move through it as you planned without too many diversions. In the example above, it's clear that pricing will be covered last and it's obvious why that's the case. In addition, the customer knows we will be presenting possible solutions above and beyond what was asked for, as well as why.

Don't hide your process from your customer. As long as the process also serves the needs and benefits of the customer, you can find ways to share and explain the steps in a way that is completely legitimate and understandable. If your current process does not benefit the customer in some way at each step, redesign your sales process.

Purposeful

Each step in the sales process should be done with purpose. As we move forward through the tasks we perform, we must understand the difference between purpose and function. The function is what we do, the purpose is why we do it. The function completes the task, the purpose achieves the goal. Both are necessary to move forward, but the most common to be absent is purpose. Can a receptionist answer and direct calls badly? Can a shared ride driver get you from point A to point B while delivering a poor experience? Can a salesperson demonstrate a product and provide information while boring their customer? The answer to all three of these is, "Yes indeed." These are clear examples of function without purpose.

As you move forward through the sales process, be purposeful. Ask yourself every step of the way, "How do I want my customer to feel while I do this?" Hopefully your answers to this question are, "excited, involved, engaged, intrigued, and happy." not, "bored, impatient, frustrated, and confused." Suffice it to say that each step in your process has a purpose that benefits the customer. By tapping into this, we change the experience for the better and STEP forward in the sales process more smoothly. Again, if the steps in your sales process do not have a purpose that benefits your customer, change your sales process!

INTERMEDIATE GOALS

As the steps to the sales process are widely different from industry to industry, as well as variable based on the nature of the business, I do not intend to provide you with a perfect model of a sales process. My primary goal here is to introduce the idea that no matter what your process is, you must move through the steps (and micro-steps) intentionally. The **Recommendations** we make are often pre-ordained by our sales process. As an example, if I have a five-step sales process, and I am currently working with a customer on step three, what do you think my upcoming **Recommendation** is going to be? Yep, you guessed it! "I **Recommend** we move to step four!"

Assuming the sales process is also good for the customer, this provides us with exciting opportunities to use R7. In the many industries in which I've worked, I've created well-defined consultation processes. With a process mapped out, we always know where we are with a customer and where we would like to guide the customer next. However, knowing what **Recommendation** you will be making doesn't mean you are ready to make it. Remember, we must have a **Reason** to make our **Recommendation** and it is always much more meaningful when these **Reasons** have been explicitly stated or agreed upon by the customer. There are a finite number of **Recommendations** we will make, and therefore a finite set of **Reasons** to make them. With this in mind, I conduct **Research** surrounding these **Reasons**. Let me lay this out for you:

- The sales process has a finite set of "steps."
- At each stage of the process, the goal is to **Recommend** the next step.
- There are specific, valid **Reasons** for a customer to take this next step.
- The purpose of **Research** is to find out which of these **Reasons** is valid for this customer.

When we practice "Outcome Orientation," we break down our entire process into a set of intermediate goals which are often chronological. While there are a multitude of ways to break down or otherwise describe a particular sales process, a generic five-step, retail sales process might look something like this:

1. Meet and Greet
2. Needs Assessment
3. Product Selection
4. Product Presentation
5. Close

Within and between these intermediate goals are a set of micro-steps we must accomplish in order to maximize our chances of successfully moving forward in the process. We can't just move from step one to step two arbitrarily. There are things we must accomplish during step one that allow us to move to step two. During the entire process, an overarching goal is to relate to the customer as a human being (**R**apport). Let's look at some of the micro-steps in between the larger framework of this particular sales process:

1. Meet and Greet
   - Establish **R**apport and relate
   - Describe the sales process (explicitly)
   - Discover **R**easons to move forward to needs assessment via **R**esearch
   - Move forward to the needs assessment intentionally with a **R**ecommendation

2. Needs assessment
   - Continue to relate and be yourself
   - Explore the customer's needs and desires (solving a problem, satisfying a desire, or both)
   - Discover both logical **R**easons and emotional **R**ewards to move on to product/service selection
   - Move forward to product or service selection intentionally with a **R**ecommendation

3. Product Selection
   - Continue to relate and be yourself
   - Explore products and services that meet the client's needs and desires
   - Continue to discover logical **Reasons** and emotional **Rewards**
   - Narrow down product selection via intentional **Recommendation**

4. Product Presentation
   - Continue to relate and be yourself
   - Present products conversationally through the lens of **Reasons** and **Rewards** (More on this in the LIVE Your Product section in Part Two (Chapter Eight)
   - Confirm product details (options, dates, accessories, etc.)
   - Move to the Close via intentional **Recommendation**

5. Close
   - Continue to relate and be yourself
   - Explain and confirm pricing
   - Obtain final commitment via **Recommendation**
   - Provide advice and direction on next steps; make this easy!
   - Move forward to **Relationship**

Yes, "relate and be yourself," is part of every step. Please remember, however, that it's not about oversharing and it's not all about you. Simple statements throughout the sales process like, "I have one of these myself," or, "I'd love to use this product at home, I only get to use it here in the showroom," are all that's required to show your human side. *Just be sure that what you share is true.*

Once you have defined the steps of your process as I have above, it will become extremely apparent "in the moment" with each customer just where you are in the process and where you need to go next. Using "Outcome Orientation" and employing the STEP method helps us intentionally move forward in the sales process efficiently and effectively.

FORWARDING THE SALES PROCESS

As you've no doubt come to understand, consultative selling isn't one big pitch at the end, it's a series of small **R**ecommendations that add up to a complete sale; small pieces that add up to the whole package. When this is done properly, the customer has made a series of small choices based on your solid advice. At the end of the sales process, all you have to do is reconfirm their choices and then describe the process to complete the purchase (with a final **R**ecommendation to move forward).

Just remember to STEP forward!

Strategic
- Have a plan. Share the plan. Follow the plan. Between the major steps of your process, be aware of the micro-steps that enable you to move forward.

Timely
- It's too early if you don't have **R**easons to move forward and haven't attempted to make a human connection.
- It's too late if you've given out too much information or invited distraction and diversion by revealing too much or asking the wrong question.

Explicit
- Don't keep your process a secret. Describe your process to your customer so they know what's coming. Use a "Recommendation Statement" to move from step to step. In this way, the customer always has logical and emotional incentives to move forward.

Purposeful
- Each task within your process also has a purpose. What you are doing is valuable for the customer and you are doing it with their goals in mind. How do you want your customer to feel as you complete these tasks?

Once you embrace the idea that you are responsible for moving through this process intentionally, you will begin to rely on **Research** as your primary tool. Remember, once you know where you want to guide your customer, all you need are **Reasons** to **Recommend** going there. You discover **Reasons** through **Research**.

> ### Key Takeaways – Chapter Five
> - **STEP Forward: Strategic, Timely, Explicit, Purposeful.**
> - As the consultant, advisor, and guide, you must lead the process intentionally.
> - **Recommendations** are the key to moving through each step of your sales process.
> - Your customers must be aware of, and comfortable with, your intended sales process.

CHAPTER SIX
PREACH LUXURY

"Any brand, product, or service can be elevated through human interaction regardless of competitive positioning. Every customer interaction has the potential to be a premium luxury experience."

PREACH LUXURY

P | **PROACTIVE**
Be an advocate for your customer. Do more than is asked, before you are asked.

R | **REAL**
Be genuine, human, and transparent. Enjoy your time with your customer.

E | **EASY**
Simplify, prepare, and coordinate your efforts. Don't make your customer wait.

A | **ACCOMMODATING**
Customize and tailor the experience. Be aware. Take action.

C | **CONSISTENT**
Be consistently amazing between people, events, and experiences.

H | **HUMAN**
You are the "they" in the stories your customers tell. Be yourself. Be exceptional.

WHY PREMIUM? WHY LUXURY?

The Seven Rs of Selling is a consultative and experiential sales methodology. When we embrace this concept, we accept that a huge part of value creation for our customers is the shopping and purchase experience all by itself. Once you begin using R7 as a strategy, you will incorporate STEP Forward to move through your sales process intentionally. The next challenge will be to upgrade your customer's experience. In this chapter, I will introduce you to the critical elements of a premium luxury experience and provide an understanding of just how these components come together to add tremendous value to the products and services you sell.

CAUTION! You may be thinking, "But I don't represent a luxury brand, product, or service. Why do I need to read a chapter about luxury?" Please be aware that many luxury experiences happen where and when you least expect them. A huge part of providing a luxury experience is finding a way to exceed your customer's expectations.

In most cases, this is much easier in a non-luxury brand where the customer's expectations are lower out of the gate. Ask yourself, what would happen if you treated someone buying a used car for $9,500 as if they were buying a $500,000 Rolls Royce? As you will see in this chapter, it would make a giant impact on the customer's experience, add tremendous value to the overall transaction and increase your chances of repeat and referral business down the road. You don't have to represent a luxury product or service to be able to increase the value of you, your offering, and your organization, because luxury is more about how you feel than it is about what you get. Even everyday commodity widgets can be sold in a luxury way. What is the beautiful and exciting part of all this? Providing this experience for our customers often costs nothing!

Let's explore the value of creating a luxury experience for our customers. When a customer has a good experience, the value of the product or service we represent increases while, simultaneously, the price of the product or service becomes less important. In short, when you provide a fantastic experience, you have the pleasure of working with a happy customer. Here are some of the benefits of working with a satisfied customer who values your product or service more, and is less sensitive to price:

- Higher closing percentages
- Larger average transactions
- Higher margins
- More repeat and referral business
- Enhanced online reputation
- Greater brand awareness
- Higher brand value
- More enjoyable experience for the sales professional (higher job satisfaction)

These are just some of the most prominent and tangible benefits. There are plenty more! At this point in this chapter, I'm hoping you are thinking, "OK, I get the value of providing a luxury experience, but how do I go about it?" Throughout the rest of this chapter, I'll introduce and explain these elements as well as provide you with examples of how they may be used.

PREACH LUXURY

In countless workshops I've conducted with customer service and sales professionals across many industries, I've asked participants to share stories about experiences they've had that exemplify luxury. As a group, we then try to extract the most common elements of these experiences and, over time, I've gathered these together. To help you remember the different keys to providing a premium luxury experience, I've created the PREACH model:

- Luxury is **Proactive**
- Luxury is **Real**
- Luxury is **Easy**
- Luxury is **Accommodating**
- Luxury is **Consistent**
- Luxury is **Human**

Let's discuss these one by one and see some examples of how they materialize in real-life situations.

LUXURY IS PROACTIVE

In almost every story told of an exceptionally positive experience, someone is "exceeding expectations," or "going above and beyond." By its very nature, this requires a proactive approach to the customer experience. Doing something more than is asked, and providing something greater than is expected, demands that we intentionally consider the customer's unique personality and situation and creatively deliver something more. Individuals who do this consistently are always on the lookout, with a keen sense of awareness of any possible opportunity to elevate their customer's experience. At the very least, we must do what we've previously agreed to do (whether organizationally or individually) before the customer has to ask, demand, or beg for something that was promised to them.

Unfortunately, many organizations and individuals fail at this last part. As a consultant, I travel quite a bit for a living. To put this in perspective, I live in North Carolina. I'm currently writing this sentence while in a hotel in New Jersey. Within the next six weeks, I'll be in Madison, Dallas, Vancouver, Philadelphia, Chicago, Atlanta, and DC. To put it mildly, I rack up quite a few air miles. My status on the airline of my choice is one of the highest possible, and I get quite a few perks when I fly with them. A few years ago, I received a letter congratulating me on my status and introducing me to a new perk. I don't remember the exact language, but it went something like this: "Thank you for your loyalty to our airline. As a member of such high status, we want you to have the best possible experience on our airline. When you fly with us, we are going to try to upgrade you to first class every chance we get. When we aren't able to upgrade you, we still want you to have a first-class experience. When you are seated in our coach cabin, we will be happy to accommodate you with anything from our food and beverage cart at no charge." Previous to this, when I was in the coach cabin, which was most of the time, I would have to pay for any food or premium beverage items.

Having received this letter, I thought, "That's fantastic." Unfortunately, the experience that went along with this new perk left a lot to be desired. The very next time I was seated in coach, I tried it out. The flight attendant asked if I wanted anything, and I said, "Yes, I'll have a cheese plate and a beer." And she said, "That will be $16." I then explained that I'd received a letter, and I was a high-status member and said, "I think it's supposed to be free." She looked at her passenger list and said, "Yeah, ok." Meanwhile, the other passengers around me were giving me dirty looks and probably thinking, "What an ass." What was supposed to be a luxury perk had turned into a horrible and embarrassing experience.

About 20 percent of the time, this experience is quite the opposite. Upon reaching my row, the flight attendant says, "Mr. Van Order?" and I say, "Yes." At which point, they say something like, "I just wanted to thank you for your loyalty to our airline and for being an elite member. We certainly appreciate you. Is there anything you'd like from our food and beverage cart? Complimentary, of course." And I say, "Yes, please. I'll have a cheese plate and a beer." When this happens, the passengers around me often say, "Wow, that's nice." I like to believe that they are thinking, "Ooh, who's that guy?" It makes me feel like a real, "baller." This is a much better experience and much more in line with what the airline intended.

This is the difference between proactively providing a luxury experience and merely reacting to what our customers ask for. When we have to ask for it, beg for it or demand it, it ceases to be a luxury experience. Due to the inconsistency of my experience with this airline, I've learned not to order anything, or just pay the $16 if they aren't proactively offering. It's just not worth it. I don't blame the flight attendants. They have a lot on their plates, and their primary concern is safety, not luxury. I do believe if they understood the night and day difference between these experiences, they would be motivated to provide a more proactive experience for their elite passengers. It would be both effortless and costless - and much more enjoyable for both parties.

How do we apply this concept to a sales situation? There are three different aspects involved when being proactive in a sales situation. First, we must be aware of the promises our organization makes to our customers via marketing, promotion, advertising, and literature. This includes our organization's website and social media, as well as any public mission or vision statements. As an example, Starbucks' mission statement is, "To inspire and nurture the human spirit - one person, one cup and one neighborhood at a time." To deliver on this mission, Starbuck's employees must understand that part of the customer experience is to deliver on this promise.

Imagine seeing an online ad for a $79 oil change (no coupon necessary). When you arrive, the attendant tells you it will be $109. You say, "I saw it for $79 online!" The attendant then says, "Yeah, ok, we'll do it for $79." This is another example of a reactive, negative experience rather than a proactive, luxury experience. The experience is ruined, and the organization's credibility is diminished. This same kind of thing happens in many industries every day. If you take the time to understand what your organization promotes and promises, you can then deliver these promotions and promises proactively, rather than wait for the customer to ask, demand or beg.

You might believe that the attendant above, who is a commissioned employee, should only do the $79 oil change when a customer indicates they know about it. This will increase commissions for the sales professional when they have customers that haven't seen the ad online. I understand this thought process, and I realize how hard it might be for a front-line employee to sacrifice a short-term commission for the long-term loyalty of a customer. However, I absolutely believe it is the right thing to do. When our pay plans are in direct conflict with the best possible customer experience, it creates inconsistency, and future customer loyalty suffers. If you need to have a separate discounted price, use a printable coupon. This way the customer will be likely to present it before the issue above has a chance to occur.

The second way to be proactive for our customers is to be completely prepared for each "next step" in the process. What can you prepare in advance of your time with the customer? What **R**esearch can you do to prepare yourself? What data do you have about the customer's history with your company? What can you find out about your customer's industry, situation, challenges, goals, competitors, and partners? I'll spend more time on this in the "Luxury is Easy" section of this chapter. As you can imagine, your proactive preparation for each step in the process makes the customer's experience so much easier.

The third way to be proactive in a sales situation is to listen well and be hyperaware of any opportunities to go "above and beyond" for our customers. Consider the following phone dialogue:

Scenario One

"Hi Mrs. Rodriguez, this is Neil at ACME Insurance, I'm just calling to confirm our appointment today at 11 a.m."

"Oh. Hi Neil, Is that today? I guess that is today! You'll have to forgive me. I haven't had my coffee yet this morning."

"That's ok, Mrs. Rodriguez. Are we still on for 11:00?"

"Yes, I'll see you then, Neil."

"Great, see you then."

Did you see the opportunity to elevate this customer's experience? Let's take a look at what Neil could have done:

Scenario Two

"Hi Mrs. Rodriguez, this is Neil at ACME Insurance, I'm just calling to confirm our appointment today at 11 a.m."

"Oh. Hi Neil, Is that today? I guess that is today! You'll have to forgive me. I haven't had my coffee yet this morning."

"That's ok, Mrs. Rodriguez. I've had two cups myself already. How do you take your coffee?

"At home I drink it black, but I'm a sucker for a vanilla latte."

"That sounds like it must be pretty good, I've never had one. Are we still on for 11?"

"Yes, I'll see you then, Neil."

"Great, see you then. And Mrs. Rodriguez?"

"Yes?"

"I'll have a vanilla latte waiting for you when you get here."

"Thanks Neil, you're the best!"

This is what hyperawareness looks like. It may sound simple to you. It may seem basic. I can honestly tell you, without hesitation, that sales professionals miss these opportunities by the droves. Being proactive about the customer experience allows us to discover and act upon these opportunities in real time. When we are proactive, we are better prepared, we save our customer's time, we adapt to their needs and wants without them having to ask, and we make things easier for them. Hyperawareness is the key to getting this right, and I'll discuss this in greater detail when I show you how to READ Your Customer (Chapter 7).

LUXURY IS REAL

Luxury isn't merely the language we use when we speak to our customers, nor is it just about what we do for them. Remember, the experience of luxury is more about how we feel than it is about what we get. When I ask people to describe the critical moments of their experiences, they inevitably describe a moment in which they felt genuinely cared for:

"I really felt like she cared about me."

"They were genuinely excited for me."

"I could tell that they really wanted to help me."

"He was enjoying helping me just as much as I was enjoying my shopping experience."

In Chapter Two, when I discussed **R**apport, I spoke about making a genuine, truthful connection with another human being. Assuming you like people and care about them, all you have to do is be yourself. When it comes to providing a fantastic experience for our clients, I'll stand by the same words I used earlier; if you have to act like you care, you are likely in the wrong profession. For some people, caring for others comes extremely naturally while, for others, it requires a bit of "reframing" their professional goals.

The sales quotas, targets, and goals we are pushed to achieve are rarely ever about genuinely caring for others. No, our objectives are almost always numeric; units, dollars, volume, margins, and averages. What if we looked at it as, "Most people cared for?" As long as we can agree that your products and services are solving problems and satisfying desires, then I'm sure we can agree that the more units you are selling, the more people and organizations you are helping. When we are genuinely caring for our customers, we elevate the experience and become more successful at the same time. How do you define success? I challenge you to measure your success by the feelings of the people you are helping. The dollars will follow.

This real, genuine concern shows up in many ways: our tone of voice, our enthusiasm, our patience, the way we listen to our customers, the questions we ask, and the small things we do. One example recently shared with me was a customer at a local furniture store. While "browsing," she saw a sofa on clearance that she really wanted to bring home the same day. She explained this to the salesperson; however, the delivery schedule was at least a week out. With the customer's permission, the representative called the Home Depot nearby and reserved a truck for the customer. Later that evening, the sales rep called the customer at home to make sure everything had gone well. Total time spent by the sales representative to elevate this experience? 10 minutes. Total cost? $0. The value of this experience? Priceless. This approach was both real and proactive.

Ultimately, we simply cannot "fake" a genuine concern for our customers. For some, it's natural. For others, it requires a bit of redefinition and reframing. For yet others, it simply isn't in the cards. In a sales or customer service position, you're allowed to have a bad day once in a very long while. If every day is a bad day, you've chosen the wrong career.

LUXURY IS EASY

The experience should be as easy as possible for your customers. When describing impressive experiences, consumers often verbalize them with words like smooth, simple, seamless, effortless, and painless. In short, *easy*. Experiential selling is a service in and of itself, and we have the responsibility of doing all we can to remove the "burden of purchasing," from our customer. For proof of this concept, look at the examples demonstrated by some of the world's most successful "disruptors:" ridesharing companies; online shopping giants; companies that deliver packaged recipes and ingredients directly to your home; and grocery stores that have your groceries ready for pickup or delivery; these are just a few examples. In spite of this trend in digitalization and automation, there remains a multitude of situations where human-to-human contact is inevitably necessary, and even preferred.

As service and sales organizations begin the evolution of infrastructure and processes, we often find hybrid systems in which a portion of the experience is digital, and the remainder is human. This disruption is affecting many industries. It's diminishing the value and pointing out the flaws in our older, outdated sales models.

In the introduction to this book, I spoke of margin compression and the overall reduction in price variation among competitors. In this new paradigm, price is no longer the decision factor for many consumers. In situations where price is similar among competitors, the experience becomes all-important, and time and convenience become key factors that sway consumer decisions.

In my experience, there are four factors that influence the ease of an experience: simplification, preparation, coordination, and efficiency. Imagine what it would be like for you, as a consumer, if you went through a shopping and purchase experience where:

- Everything was simplified and uncomplicated. This includes the process, product selection, available information, proposals, pricing, and payment processing. Instead of making you fill out paperwork, they prepared it in advance. You didn't have to do anything that someone in the organization could have done for you.

- At each step, the individuals you were dealing with were well prepared. All the information you had previously provided was put to good use. Everything was ready for your experience.
- All the individuals you had to deal with coordinated their efforts. You never had to repeat yourself or provide the same information a second time. Anything you had done digitally translated seamlessly to the human side of the experience as people became part of the process. Your decisions, preferences, desires, issues, and concerns were communicated behind the scenes, and each person in the chain picked right up where the last left off.
- The experience was smooth and efficient, and you didn't spend any of your precious time waiting. It might have taken some time, but that time was spent productively.

Luckily for us, most of these aspects are controlled by people. Individually, we have a lot of power to enhance these aspects of our customer's experiences. By doing so, we create more value in ourselves and our organizations, as well as our products and services. Let's take another look at these aspects individually:

Simplification

"Take a walk" through your existing process, as would a customer, and identify places where you could simplify things. Are there barriers to moving forward that don't need to be there? Are there things we could do for the customer instead of asking them to do them? Below is a recent dialogue between myself and another individual on a business-related social media site. He reached out to me to solicit his services, and I was legitimately interested. This conversation took place via email exchange (and his name was not Joe).

> "Hi Hans, glad we connected ... (Insert sales pitch here). How does your schedule look over the next few days to chat?"
>
> "Hi Joe. Your message is timely. Why don't we plan a quick chat on Monday around 2pm Eastern?"
>
> "Sounds good. Can you go to my booking calendar and reserve that time

slot? Go to (weblink provided) and select "strategy session." Cheers!"

As you might suspect, I chose not to click the link and book the "strategy session." To my surprise, Joe never followed up with me. You might argue that providing me with a link to book my own appointment was *easy*. In my mind, I had already said, "yes" to his request to "chat." I had also provided the date and time. I can't speak for you, but saying yes and finding 30 minutes to have a conversation with someone trying to sell me something was *hard* for me. Have you ever been on the brink of a purchase when an inconvenience in the process caused you to give up? The decision to move to the next step is hard enough for our customers. Any hiccup along the way, could be the reason they say, "this just isn't worth it." This is precisely what happened to me here. In my mind, what I should have received was an invite to add the meeting to my calendar with a "thank you."

Preparation

The best way to understand this is to consider how you might prepare for a job interview at a company you would love to work for. Would you show up and "wing it," or would you scour all available sources of information and get yourself ready? What's their dress code? What is their mission? How are they competitively positioned? What's been said about them in the press? Who are their biggest competitors? How are their future goals related to your talents and aspirations? In effect, you are preparing for a sales process. Are you not planning to influence and persuade them you are the right person for the job? Would you assume they will have printed your resume, or will you bring one with you?

I am sometimes asked, "What should I prepare?" The answer is simple, "Everything you can, everything appropriate to the situation, and everything you have time for." Are your customers coming to see specific products? Are those products positioned in the right place, clean and ready to be demonstrated to the finest level possible? Is there paperwork that can be filled out in advance? Are there others involved in this process you could call or converse with to coordinate your efforts better? Do you have a list of questions prepared? Do you have some **R**ecommendations handy – with **R**easons and **R**ewards to go with them? In essence, get the stuff ready, stage the product, fill out the paperwork, make the calls, and do the **Research**. Consider the following dialogue:

"Welcome, Mr. & Mrs. Williams, my name's Kevin. We spoke on the phone?"

"Yes, hello Kevin."

"After our call, I reached out to your general contractor and your designer to get a better understanding of your project. You certainly are building a beautiful outdoor kitchen. I'm a little jealous, to be honest."

"Thank you, we're pretty excited about it, too."

"Your designer, Tina, emailed me a copy of the design, so I have accurate measurements of everything. She also told me not to let you leave today without selecting a sink to go with your countertops."

"That sounds like her; she told us the same thing."

"Based on my call with your general contractor, I understand that a large portion of your countertop will be in direct sunlight?"

"Yes, that's true. It will be in the shade after about 2pm, but before that, it's directly in the sun."

"With that in mind, I've chosen a selection of stone for your countertops that will be more heat tolerant and minimize expansion and contraction. I'll show you some of our best outdoor-rated material. I would also suggest we focus on the lighter colors so you won't have to worry about it getting too hot to the touch."

"That sounds great. Thank you."

"My pleasure. Tina asked me to show you three of her favorite choices for your sink, but I think it would be best to choose your stone first. Since I have the dimensions, I can show you where the seams will be, and I'll also be able to price everything out for you to help make your final decisions."

"That's perfect. Thank you again."

"Absolutely, it's why I'm here. When we're done today, I'll make sure Tina has all the specs, and we'll coordinate our efforts with your contractor. Once the cabinets are in, we can template everything and then cut the stone to exact measurements."

Ask yourself, what would this sales process have looked and sounded like without the preparation done by the sales consultant? Kevin is making everything extremely smooth and easy for his customers. Do you see the elements of **R**esearch, **R**apport, **R**easons, **R**ecommendations, and **R**ewards? Has Kevin effectively leveraged this customer's relationship with their contractor and designer, Tina? Preparation is obviously a key factor when making things easier for our customers.

Coordination

Another element of a smooth experience is coordination. This is where we connect our human efforts with our digital capabilities and honor the preferences of our customers. This is where we give our customers credit for everything they've already done, the information they've already provided, and questions they've already answered. This is where we collaborate with other members of our team and choreograph the customer's experience. When we coordinate our efforts, the customer never has to repeat themselves or "start over" with the next person in the chain.

Increasingly, we are working with customers who have completed a portion of the sales process digitally. They've made product selections on our website, indicated preferences, provided information, answered questions, and filled out forms. As organizations struggle to keep up with technology and customer preferences, there is often a disconnect between the digital experience and the human experience. With technology "up and running," we think we've modernized our business processes. But, in reality, once human contact is made, our customer goes through a time warp because we haven't updated our human behaviors so that they coordinate with the digital experience. They are then forced to begin again in an outdated analog process. The experience suffers, value diminishes, and price sensitivity increases.

To combat this, we have to be willing to deconstruct and reconstruct both our online and offline processes. Once we have the framework in place, we then fill in the human behaviors that support this combined process. In most of the organizations I've worked with, this is much easier said than done. Building it all from scratch would be so much easier than going through the adaptations and modifications necessary to keep pace with the new consumer environment. After recommending specific fundamental changes to many different business owners, and meeting quite a bit of resistance, I've often asked them, "If you were building it all from scratch, would you build it the way you have it now, or the way I'm recommending?" They inevitably admit that they would follow my recommendation. The issue isn't that we don't see where we need to go. The pain stems from trying to get there from where we are.

Excellent examples of this concept are often found in industries and organizations where they begin their sales process with "an appointment focus:" insurance, real estate, automotive, fitness centers, and countless others. Once they receive an opportunity or "lead," they reach out to the prospective consumer attempting to set up a face-to-face appointment. This is usually an extremely effective strategy, which I myself have taught to many individuals and organizations. A face-to-face meeting is often extremely beneficial for both the consumer and the sales organization. Unfortunately, in an increasingly digital age where consumers are more and more willing to complete transactions sight unseen, this strategy must be modified to coincide with our digital presence. A growing number of customers across varied industries are searching for ways to complete transactions without meeting anyone face-to-face. Where this is a requirement, they are attempting to take the transaction as far as they can before they commit to a meeting.

Many of these organizations have invested in infrastructure and hired teams of people dedicated to managing these opportunities and setting up appointments for them. The pay plans of these individuals are often based on the number of appointments they successfully influence. Simultaneously, these same organizations have invested in technology, enabling consumers to move further and further down the sales process without physically traveling to the business location. The combination of these two sales systems colliding can best be described as "The Clash of the Titans." The human process is fighting against the digital process and, once again, the customer experience is suffering. While we work through this evolution, many organizations are finding that a modern digital process combined with a hybrid human process is the right combination. In essence, the digital side is fully modern and capable, while the human side readily adapts to the digital "history" of a customer, "on the fly" when necessary.

In the above example, a representative may recommend an on-site appointment. They may also promote a more digital route, for example using the company's website. As soon as the customer indicates a preference for a more remote transaction, the focus shifts immediately to a modern, streamlined, and more digital approach. Furthermore, all on-site representatives are proactively discovering whether or not a consumer has a "digital history" in order to pivot if necessary, preventing the necessity to start over from the beginning.

The other aspect of coordination is human-to-human. Consider the following dialogue:

Scenario One

"Hello, how can we help you today?"

"I have an appointment at 2:30 with Michelle."

"Ok, have a seat, I'll see if I can find her for you."

Scenario Two

"Hello, how can we help you today?"

"I have an appointment at 2:30 with Michelle."

"Yes, hello, you must be Mrs. Warnes. Michelle's expecting you. Please have a seat, and I'll let her know you're here."

This is coordination at work. In the first few seconds of this customer's visit, she knows that she is important to the organization. She feels they are prepared to work with her, and she knows that they communicated with each other and work as a team. If we expand this to include all customer interactions with each of the individuals in our organization, the experience is elevated exponentially.

Efficiency

The last aspect necessary to create an easy experience for our customers is efficiency. I highly encourage you to do your best to create a "no wait," sales process. This doesn't mean you have to do everything extremely quickly, but it does mean that you have to eliminate portions of your sales process that make it necessary for your customer to wait…for anything.

I love it when someone asks me, "Would you like to wait?" My initial response, (mostly in my head…but sometimes not) is, "Of course not, does anyone?" No one wants to wait. Waiting always diminishes the value of your product or service. Have you ever walked into a place of business, taken one look at the line, and walked right back out? Sure, you have. Everyone has. When you did this, you mentally calculated the value of what you were going to get, and decided that it's not worth the wait.

There is a restaurant near us that has excellent food, an amazing atmosphere, and outstanding service. I absolutely hate going there. They don't take reservations, and you can't call ahead. They don't use or accept any apps that enable you to "get in line" without physically being there. It is old school; first come, first served. It's not worth the wait. Do you want another example? Look no further than your local department of motor vehicles. The antithesis of the luxury experience. My favorite part? After I've wasted almost an entire day in "line A," I get to move directly to "line B."

This type of scenario is not limited to this institution. I see it every day in many of the organizations I work with. Just ask a sales professional that also has a "finance department." Yep, line A, line B. In many of these situations, I work with the organization to condense these functions or create a "parallel process." Instead of having a linear process, in which the customer has to wait for another individual to be available, or wait while paperwork is prepared, we engage the customer in a necessary part of the purchase or acquisition process during the time they would otherwise be waiting. It takes coordination, as mentioned earlier, and it takes time to get it right; but believe me, it's worth the wait!

LUXURY IS ACCOMMODATING

When we have a truly luxurious experience, we want to believe that this isn't the same experience everyone else receives. We want to feel special and unique. The recognition of a truly bespoke, tailored, personalized, and customized experience goes a long way toward value creation. When we recognize something unique and different about a customer or their situation and proactively modify the experience, we make a change or addition that is customized and meaningful to them. They feel accommodated.

By definition, to make an accommodation for someone is to do something for them, "outside the norm." In my mind, there are two ways to accomplish this. The first is to literally do something out of the ordinary. I call this "Awareness and Action." The second method requires us to put a unique spin on our routine tasks or standard operating procedure. I call this "Situational Tailoring." Let's take a look at each of these:

"Awareness and Action"

The first step here is to become aware of something tangible about our customers and take action based on that awareness. This allows us to differentiate the process and go "above and beyond." The moment we start to see, hear, or feel friction with a client is the moment we should consider adapting our process.

This could be the consultant who notices their customers becoming frustrated with their children, and helps them relax by creatively finding a way to occupy and entertain the children. Or it might be a sales professional who offers to provide services outside of regular business hours when their customer expresses difficulty with the schedule. Here are a few more examples:

- Bringing the product to the customer instead of forcing the customer to come to them.
- Offering a preliminary "site visit" because the customer isn't sure about the details and doesn't want it to go wrong.

- Noticing that it's close to the customer's birthday and getting them a card and a cake.
- Giving a customer who is purchasing a knife set a personal recipe to try at home.
- Performing a detailed analysis of a business to business (B2B) customer's previous year's sales to support the purchase of a new machine or technology. Nothing elevates a customer's experience more than doing the unexpected and seizing an opportunity based on something seen, heard, or remembered.

"Situational Tailoring"

Often we structure our sales process with the aim of providing a premium experience to our customers. Indeed, many organizations pride themselves on the very idea of luxury. When our everyday process offers a premium experience to everyone, how do we accommodate them? How do we personalize and customize this experience? To accomplish this, we need to separate *what* we are doing and saying with *how* we are doing and saying it. We have to pay attention to our language and our behavior. I call this "Situational Tailoring."

Many organizations have a "give away" of some kind during the sales process. This could be as simple as providing a refreshment, catalog, brochure, or a "goody bag." When we use "Situational Tailoring," we pay close attention to *how* we provide this small take away. Instead of saying, "Would you like a coffee?" we say, "Let me get you a beverage. Would you prefer something hot or cold?" Here are some other examples:

- Instead of, "Would you like a brochure to take with you?" we say, "I circled a few items in our brochure for you based on our conversation." The key words in this sentence are "I" and "for you." Remember, we are transforming sales into a service.
- Instead of staging the "goody bags" where your customers can see them, (indicating that everyone gets one), keep them out of sight and make it personal with, "I wanted you to have this." You get bonus points if you use "Awareness and Action" to customize the contents. This is leagues better than, "Be sure to grab one of our thank you gifts on the way out."

Additionally, we use "Situational Tailoring" every time we use R7. If you follow *The Seven Rs of Selling*, you will make a series of **R**ecommendations based on the customer's personal **R**easons, and you will be reinforcing your **R**ecommendations with emotionally unique **R**ewards. As long as you are using the correct language as you do this, your customers will perceive an elevated level of service. Again, the key words in this exchange will be "I" and "you."

LUXURY IS CONSISTENT

While a consistently premium experience is beneficial to value creation throughout the sales process, it is even more critical to loyalty, referrals, and repeat business in the future. There are two facets of consistency I would like to focus on: consistency between employees and departments; and consistency between events and experiences. Having a consistent experience between employees and departments typically enhances the overall value during a single buying cycle. A consistent experience between events and experiences increases the value of working with you and your organization over the long-term, through multiple buying cycles.

Consistency among employees and departments

When we are impressed by one individual, we give credit to that individual. When we are impressed with multiple people in the same organization, we give credit to the organization. Disney is an excellent example of this. I don't often hear, "Wow, that one particular Cast Member at Disney was amazing." Instead, I hear about the overall experience of Disney as a whole. One staff member being helpful is nice; having a fantastic experience with a whole team of people elevates the entire organization in the eyes of the customer.

Earlier, I wrote that luxury is *easy*, and I discussed the importance of coordination. I talked about collaborating with other team members and choreographing the experience for the customer. This applies to the sharing of information, so there is no repetition or starting over, as well as the consistency of enthusiasm, language, attitude, and empowerment among employees. This also applies to the consistency of our recommendations. If one person recommends that a customer do "X" and another employee or department recommends, "Y," there is a fundamental problem. This detracts from the experience, creates confusion, and reduces the customer's confidence.

An excellent example of this was displayed during a recent home purchase. The home being purchased had multiple HVAC units, which the buyer's realtor suggested should be inspected. The inspection company recommended more than $10,000 of deferred maintenance and repairs. A request was made to the seller to share in the cost of completing the work. The seller balked at this request because they had been paying to have twice-yearly visits from an HVAC company to fully maintain the system. As it turns out, the company maintaining the system and the company recommending the repairs were *the same company*. Ouch! This put the HVAC company in an impossible situation. Either they were recommending $10,000 of work that wasn't needed, or they were improperly maintaining the system.

When I am working with an organization to improve a specific aspect of their process, I often have conversations with each of the people involved. During these conversations, I ask a multitude of questions about how they handle the process as well as how they perceive others handle it. This usually shines a bright light on any discrepancies. This is an opportunity to bring them all together and map out a process everyone agrees with, creating consistency. This consistency among, and between employees and departments is the precursor to consistency between events and experiences.

Consistency among events and experiences

Loyalty to any business, whether it's B2B or B2C, begins with consistency. The reverse is also true. Inconsistency is the easiest way to decrease future loyalty. To put this in perspective, consider your favorite restaurant. Think of three reasons why it's your favorite restaurant. Chances are, you thought of things like the quality and flavors of the food, the service you receive, the ambience. If these things were different each time you went, would it continue to be your favorite? If you are anything like me, you just said to yourself, "Of course not." It all comes down to confidence and risk.

Once I realize that working with you and your organization is a consistently great experience, I gain confidence that I will always enjoy my experience with you. This *reduces* the risk of choosing you and *increases* the risk of choosing someone else. On the other hand, if I am "trying something new," every time I come in contact with you and your organization, what's to stop me from actually trying something new?

When I lived in the Pittsburgh area with my family, my wife and I frequented a seafood restaurant called Off The Hook. In addition to having a great name, they provided fantastic service, the food was consistently amazing, and the atmosphere was always pleasant. This restaurant became our default place to go for "date night." Over time, we came to know the owners, and we had a favorite bartender. Because of our consistently positive experience, it was a risk for us to go anywhere else. We did try other restaurants for variety, but often found ourselves back at Off The Hook. Over the course of two years, we must have gone at least 10 times. While I ordered one of three or four of my favorite dishes, my wife only ever ordered one dish, swordfish veracruz, extra spicy. She had ordered it during our first visit and absolutely loved it. I encouraged her to try other things, but she always told me, *"It isn't worth the risk."*

This is the most significant advantage digital processes have over human experiences. Computers are consistent. They do what they are programmed to do the same way every time. I ask people all the time if they would prefer to deal with a human or a computer. They almost always respond, "It depends on who the human is." For evidence of this, the next time you're checking out of your local grocery store, take note of how many people are using the automated check out lane. As things become increasingly digital, our job as humans is to fight this trend with our own consistency.

When consumers begin to understand that you have consistently excellent employees across departments as well as consistently excellent events and experiences, they become comfortable, and maybe even mildly addicted to you and your organization. Don't believe me? Try googling "Disney addict."

LUXURY IS HUMAN

Over the past few years, I've asked thousands of people to describe the most amazing experiences they've ever had. By a wide margin, the most common word used when describing a premium luxury experience is the word "they:"

- "**They** took care of everything."
- "**They** remembered my name and what I liked."
- "**They** were so attentive to my every need."
- "**They** treated me like I was their most important customer."
- "**They** did it without me asking."
- "**They** had it waiting for me."
- "**They** valued my time."
- "**They** really cared about me."
- "**They** were all so wonderful to work with."

Your customers are no different. They tell stories too. Please always remember, and lock this deep inside: *you* are the ***they*** in the stories your customers tell! The experience of luxury, the feeling of luxury, comes from the people, not just the product. When I ask groups to talk about amazing experiences, they speak about the people who helped them, the people they worked with, and the people who made them feel important, special, and cared for. Unfortunately, when people describe poor experiences, "they" is also the most common word used. Being human is our most significant advantage and our greatest weakness.

THE COST OF LUXURY

The provision of a premium luxury experience provides massive competitive advantages and can often be accomplished with little to no cost. As variation in price among competitors continues to decrease, the experience will continue to be a dominant factor moving forward. *Any brand, product, or service can be elevated through human interaction regardless of competitive positioning. Every customer interaction has the potential to be a premium luxury experience.* All things being equal, price will be the determining factor. Lucky for us, all things are not equal, and we are often the differentiating factor. In this chapter, I hope I've given you several ideas to enhance your process and behaviors.

LUXURY IS A HUMAN COMPETITIVE ADVANTAGE

In today's world, we are seeing a rapid increase in the automation and digitalization of sales and service systems. However, the provision of a luxury experience is where digital systems can't compete with humans. I have taught you to PREACH luxury:

- Luxury is **Proactive**
- Luxury is **Real**
- Luxury is **Easy**
- Luxury is **Accommodating**
- Luxury is **Consistent**
- Luxury is **Human**

Computers can't do this! They do only what they are programmed to do, and their ability to be proactive is minimal. By definition, computer interaction is synthetic and artificial - the very opposite of real. While working with a computer might seem easy, the moment something out of the ordinary occurs, the machine is helpless, and it becomes painful. The digital world is incapable of accommodating.

A computer cannot utilize "Awareness and Action" or "Situational

Tailoring"; there are just too many possibilities and eventualities that would need to be pre-programmed. Even the most advanced system in the world is still doing only what it is programmed to do, which means it reacts the same way for everyone in the same situation, making it the norm. Accommodating means going "above and beyond," and behaving "outside the norm." The one area where computers and programs can compete is consistency - but we take that for granted.

When a human experience is consistent, it's impressive; but a digital experience is expected to be consistent. And lastly, a digital experience can't ever be human. Would it be as meaningful if someone described an experience by saying, "The computer remembered my name and what I liked. It really cared about me?"

The ongoing "digital transformation" presents a danger to the mundane, not the exceptional. Take a look at today's thriving travel agencies. In the late 1980s, the advent of online travel booking rocked the industry. In the ensuing years, travel agencies were on the brink of extinction. Today, this industry is making a comeback - especially with the younger generations. How is this industry beginning to thrive again on a human level? By PREACHing luxury!

Key Takeaways – Chapter Six

- PREACH Luxury: Proactive, Real, Easy, Accommodating, Consistent, Human.
- A luxury experience adds value to you, your offering, and your organization.
- A luxury experience is more about how they feel than it is about what they get.
- Luxury requires preparation in advance and hyperawareness in the moment.

CHAPTER SEVEN
READ YOUR CUSTOMER

"Meaningful customer relationships and elevated customer experiences do not happen by accident."

READ YOUR CUSTOMER

R |
Discover your customer's reality and make a human connection. Share your truth.

E |
Be hyperaware and seize every opportunity to enhance your customer's experience.

A |
Provide guidance and advice in service to your customer. Solve problems and satisfy desires.

D |
Ask the right question, at the right time in the right way. Lead the conversation.

DISCOVERY AND DIRECTION

In previous chapters, you've learned the concepts of *The Seven Rs of Selling* as well as how to STEP Forward through the sales process and PREACH Luxury. These are the basic components of a consultative and experiential sales process. Using a system to provide advice; relate to your customer; lead the process with intentionality; and elevate your customer's experience, are the keys to achieving success. In this chapter, I will introduce you to a model which should help you blend these components into one seamless methodology: READ Your Customer.

As I discussed in Chapter 4, in any real-time consultative situation, you may cycle between R1 and R5 multiple times. It helps many individuals to embrace this thought process by grouping sections of the process into discovery and direction. Seek to understand and then provide guidance based on that understanding. While conducting **R**esearch, building **R**apport, and discovering **R**easons, we are in discovery mode. As we move into a "Recommendation Statement" using **R**easons, **R**ecommendation, and **R**ewards, we shift into direction. It's not a mistake that **R**easons are a part of both discovery *and* direction. During discovery, we are gathering **R**easons to help us formulate our advice, and during direction, we are stating the **R**easons back to the customer as the rationale for our **R**ecommendation.

These modes are not tied to a particular point in the sales process. They are utilized *intentionally* based on where we are in real-time with our customer. In discovery, we are asking questions and actively listening to our customer. In direction, we are providing advice, the rationale for our advice, and the emotional benefits of following this advice. When in discovery, we are helpful and curious. When in direction, we are confident, competent, and often passionate. Think about it. How do you want your attorney to act and sound as they are *discovering* your situation? How do you want them to sound when they are *directing* you to move forward?

When we use R7 in this way, we are transforming ourselves into experiential consultants rather than salespeople. When a doctor accurately diagnoses a condition and recommends surgery, do we feel like the doctor "sold" us an operation, or do we feel as if we received advice and direction?

If we want our customers to feel advised and directed, we must assume the role of an advisor, and this begins with asking good questions and giving good advice.

I have been listening to, analyzing, critiquing, and otherwise evaluating sales conversations for quite a long time. Over that time, I've come to realize that the difference between acceptable performance and exceptional performance is often decided "in the moment" with the customer. This critical moment in time is where the most talented sales professionals shine. This is where they combine, without hesitation, the experiential consulting methodology of R7 with the desire and ability to PREACH luxury. They never miss an opportunity to humanize themselves and relate to their customers on a personal level. They never miss a chance to elevate their customer's experience. They never miss an opportunity to provide meaningful and beneficial advice.

When none of those opportunities exist, they move back to discovery by asking an intelligent and well-informed question. It should come as no surprise that I've created a model to help you react appropriately in any given situation when you are interacting in real-time with your customer.

READ YOUR CUSTOMER

READ stands for Relate, Elevate, Advise, and Discover. The most talented professionals I've worked with over the years have learned to actively listen to and observe the nuances of their customers' behavior. However, they don't stop there; they have a strategy to channel what they've heard and observed into a meaningful and valuable *reaction*.

In the previous chapter, I explained how human interaction is superior to digital communication. Ironically, now I'm going to teach you to think and act a bit like a computer; its keyboard, to be specific. A computer keyboard is an "input device." It is specifically designed to receive input from a user and react to that input by displaying a character or symbol or possibly taking action (opening or closing a window, for example). When no keys are pressed, the keyboard appears dormant, but it is not. It is constantly checking to see if input has been received. This is why the computer reacts instantly when the keys are pressed. This is a simplified example but, hopefully, you get the picture. (Also, I promise that this is as technical as I'm going to get in this book.)

Similar to the keyboard, the hyperaware sales professional, through listening and observing, is constantly filtering all customer input. Now, I want you to imagine that there are only three keys on this keyboard; relate, elevate, and advise. When one of those keys is pressed, we react instantly in the appropriate way. To continue the computer analogy, here is what that program might look like in plain English (full disclosure: I'm not a computer programmer, my apologies to those of you who are).

Input Received

RELATE: Is this an opportunity to relate?

> If yes, share something personal and connect on a human level, then go to ELEVATE.
>
>> If no, go to ELEVATE.

ELEVATE: Is this an opportunity to elevate?

> If yes, elevate the customer experience by PREACHing luxury then go to ADVISE.
>
>> If no, go to ADVISE.

ADVISE: Is this an opportunity to advise?

> If yes, use **Reason** – **Recommendation** – **Reward** to provide direction, then STEP Forward.
>
>> If no, go to DISCOVER

DISCOVER: Ask a well-informed and meaningful question, then go back to RELATE.

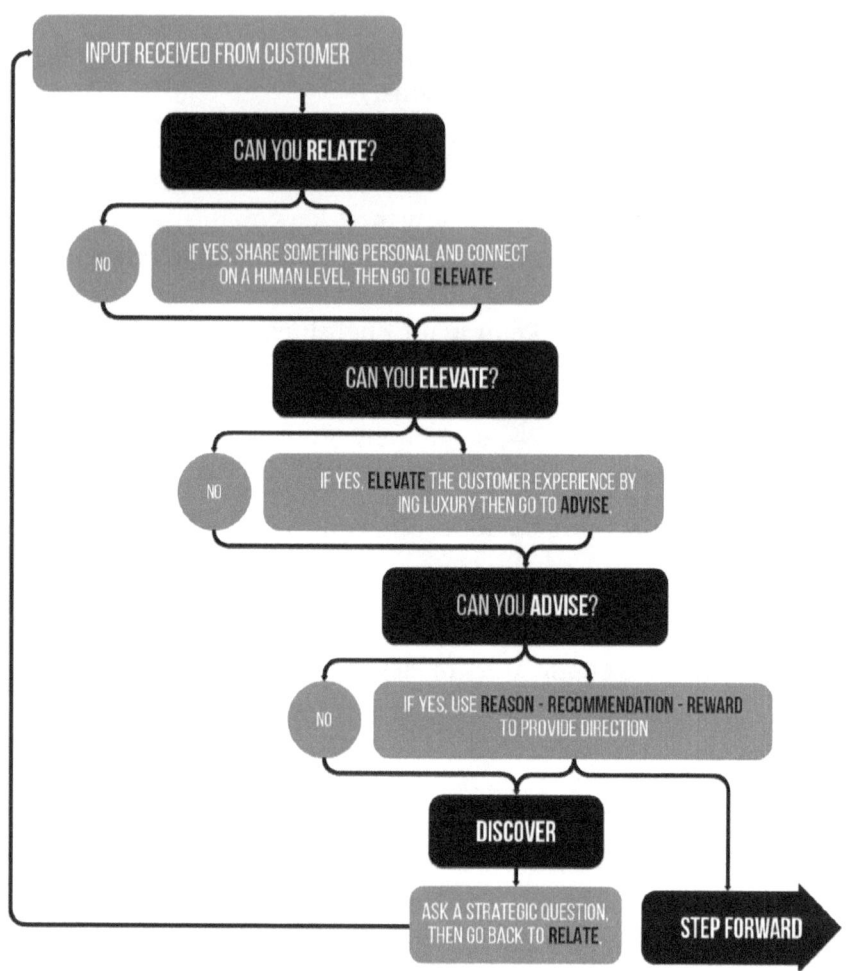

This is the "program," continually running in my brain when I am in an active conversation. This active conversation might be on the phone, in person, by email, or even text. All input filters through this mechanism. If I am on top of my game, I will never miss an opportunity to relate on a human level, elevate my customer's experience, or provide good advice.

You'll notice I said there were only three keys on the keyboard, yet there are four instructions. This is because unlike a computer keyboard, a sales professional does not go dormant and wait for input when no keys are pressed. A sales professional prompts for input by asking an intentionally designed question (**R**esearch). Stated plainly, if there are no opportunities to relate, elevate, or advise, we move to discovery. Let's take a look at each of these concepts individually:

Relate

This "instruction" is all about making a human connection with your customer on a personal level. I introduced this concept to you as the second "R" in R7. For a quick review, see the **R**apport section in Chapter Four. I will go into more depth on this strategy in Chapter 11. Building rapport is something we want to do as often, and as early as possible.

As you actively listen and observe, you are simply asking yourself, "Did my customer just say or do something that I can connect with personally?" If the answer is yes, you move in that direction by sharing something personal about yourself that relates to what they've just said. If you feel that you've already connected with them, you will decide if you want to continue to relate further or move on in the conversation. Here's a quick example:

> *"Thanks for carving out a few minutes to discuss the indications for our new antihypertensive Dr. Bowman."*
>
> *"Sure, just make it fast, I'm leaving soon to catch the last half of my son's soccer game."*
>
> *"I'll make it quick, I've got two at home myself. For us, it's hockey and dance. Let me jump right to the important stuff so you can get going. I'll also leave you some literature with the studies we conducted so you can review when you have more time."*

In this case, Dr. Bowman pressed both the relate and elevate keys, prompting our sales professional to share something personal as well as show concern for the doctor's time. If you are like most of the people that have come through our workshops, you just said to yourself, "I do that naturally all the time." My challenge to you is to review your conversations and ask yourself, "Did I share anything about myself? Did I miss any opportunities to elevate my customer's experience?" When you become aware of this, you will realize that it doesn't happen naturally all the time. READing your customer provides a system to help you do it early and often.

Elevate

To elevate, you filter what you hear and see through the PREACH Luxury model. How can you use what you just heard or observed to elevate their experience? Can you use this new data to be more **proactive**? Is this an opportunity to express **real** concern and care for your customer? Can you make this process **easier** for them based on that information? Is this a chance to **accommodate** and tailor their experience through "Awareness and Action" or "Situational Tailoring?" Did they express something that you need to share with others in your organization so you can be **consistent**? Above all things, be **human** and be yourself.

Advise

Did the last piece of information provided by the customer give you strong **Reasons** to make a **Recommendation**? Are there clear emotional **Rewards** for the customer to move forward based on your advice? Have you connected with your customer on a human level yet? Have you seized on an opportunity to elevate their experience? If the answers to these questions are yes, it's time to advise them.

We do this through the core of R7 with a **Reason** - **Recommendation** - **Reward** statement. This is where we STEP Forward correctly through the sales process. What's the next big step? Are all the micro-steps in place? The timing of our advice is critical. In a perfect scenario, we've built **Rapport** and elevated the customer's experience before we make our **Recommendation**. If our customer is enjoying their experience with us and trusts us because we have connected, it is much more likely they will follow our advice in this moment.

Discover

When our conversation "goes dormant" with our customer, unlike the keyboard we do not remain static and wait for input. We prompt the conversation forward by returning to one of our **Research** questions. Discovery combines R1, R2, and R3. **Research**, **Rapport**, and **Reasons**. In reality, it's a circular process. The READ process begins with discovery. I just couldn't bring myself to create a model in which I was instructing you to DREAD your customer, so READ it is! The moment we ask a question, we begin our **Research**. The customer's response then get's filtered through the READ model, where we relate and elevate. When the timing is right, we advise. When and if the conversation lags, we move back to discovery and begin again.

Summary

Meaningful customer relationships and elevated customer experiences do not happen by accident. **READ**ing your customer can be elevated to an art form. Employed consistently, it becomes a habit. Those that genuinely use this method stand out far above the rest. However, in my experience, I would estimate this skillset is actively utilized by less than 10 percent of the sales population. I've had thousands of conversations over my lifetime and reviewed thousands more in the course of my profession. There are so many missed opportunities!

Personally, I can no longer turn it off. The "program" is always running in my brain, even when I'm the customer. At the time of this writing, two of my sons are ten years old. As you might expect, I've shared with them some of my thoughts on how sales conversations should go. The last time I went with them to buy shoes, I had a great conversation with them on the way home.

"Dad, can you believe he didn't tell us anything about himself? I told him I played soccer, and I even said I had a game later today. He didn't even wish me good luck."

Some might say I'm creating monsters. I say I'm helping my sons connect with other human beings and exercise persuasion and influence when they are in a position to help someone.

Key Takeaways – Chapter Seven

- READ Your Customer: Relate, Elevate, Advise, Discover.
- The customer's interaction with the sales professional is the most significant element of value creation.
- The moments you spend with your customers in real-time are the most critical to overall success.
- A sales professional does not go "dormant" in a conversation. Move to discovery.

CHAPTER EIGHT
LIVE YOUR PRODUCT

"Feature – benefit – booooring!"

LIVE YOUR PRODUCT

L  **LISTEN**
Everything your customer asks or says is an opportunity to highlight your products and services.

I  **INTERACT**
Provide opportunities for your customer to experience your products or services with multiple senses.

V  **VERIFY**
Confirm the choices they've made and relate features and benefits to the wants and needs they've shared.

E  **ENGAGE**
Ask before you tell! Have a two way conversation instead of a one way presentation.

ENGAGING PRODUCT PRESENTATIONS

As you use *The Seven Rs of Selling* effectively, you will STEP forward through the sales process, PREACH luxury, and READ your customer. At some point, however, it is highly likely you will need to present your product or service to your customer. Usually, this is an educational process. Most sales training methods employ some version of feature-benefit or feature-function-benefit training. You discuss a particular feature, explain how it functions (if appropriate), and then explain how this feature and function benefits your customer. Here are a few examples:

- "This toaster has anti-jam and simple retrieval, which means your toasted items will pop up every time, elevated above the toaster body when finished so you won't burn your fingers. You will have the confidence that a wide range of items can be toasted perfectly every time. Anyone in your family will be able to use it safely and conveniently."
- "This is a smaller-bodied guitar ideal for playing fingerstyle. With Indian rosewood and solid spruce providing a rich tonal voice, it sounds and looks amazing. You're going to feel great and look fantastic while you're playing it."
- "This vehicle has anti-lock brakes that regulate brake pressure and coordinate wheel activity. This prevents lock-ups and skidding under hard braking conditions, even in slippery conditions like ice, rain, and gravel. With anti-lock brakes, you will have more control of the vehicle when braking as well as a shorter stopping distance. You will have the comfort of knowing your vehicle is safer for you and your family under extreme conditions."

There are two inherent flaws in this method. The first is most products and services have a plethora of features to discuss. The toaster, for example, also has an all-stainless exterior, a quick-release bottom tray, large slot sizes, a 'stylish appearance,' and accurate settings. The guitar has upgraded bracing, abalone trim, a hand-beveled armrest, finely calibrated tuners, and an ultra-thin gloss finish. The vehicle has more than I can count. Try to imagine the sales representative providing a feature-function-benefit presentation for each one of these features.

The second flaw is this is often a one-way diatribe of information from the sales representative to the customer. It is frequently overwhelming and usually boring. In the circles I run in, we call this "the product dump," and it is an epidemic across sales teams everywhere. *Feature - benefit - booooring!*

The solution? You must make your product presentation interactive and engaging. If there are many features to discuss, you must pick and choose the aspects of your product or service that are most appropriate and relevant to your customer.

LIVE YOUR PRODUCT

I created the LIVE model to help you deliver engaging, meaningful, and interactive product and service presentations. LIVE stands for Listen, Interact, Verify, and Engage. Active **listening** provides us with the information we need to choose the right features to discuss, as well as an understanding of how to go about engaging and involving our customers in the presentation. It is necessary to have your customers **interact** with the product through the use of their senses. If you are presenting a service, this interaction often requires sales-aides such as diagrams, flow charts, or other physical examples. There is additional value created when you **verify** the appropriateness of a feature/function for this particular customer. Lastly, **engage** requires us to make this a meaningful two-way conversation.

Listen

Throughout your ongoing conversations with your customers, you should be taking mental (and possibly physical) notes. These notes are triggers for you to remember key aspects of your customer's situation, which will help you solve problems and satisfy desires. How are these problems and desires linked to the features and benefits of your products and services? What other information have you gleaned that will help you ask well-informed questions and engage them in the product presentation?

Are you listening to your customer's questions and transforming them into opportunities to explain the competitive advantages of your products and services? On the product side, questions fall into only four basic groups; aesthetics, functionality, performance, and operation. On the service side, customer questions will point to who you typically help, what you do, and how you do it.

Interact

With physical products, take every opportunity to have your customer interact with all their senses. Be sure to describe physical characteristics as they interact. "Do you see the thickness of the hinge? Can you feel the weight and solidity of this door? Go ahead and swing it shut, listen to how smooth and quiet it is as it closes softly. Can you smell the cedar lining? Can you taste the grain of the wood?" OK, maybe not that last one, but I'm sure you get the idea. As they are interacting with the product, ask questions and provide direction so they can physically experience the features rather than listen to a monologue about how fantastic it is.

If you are discussing the features and benefits of a service or recommending a course of action, use diagrams, pictures, models, or other physical props. Have them interact with the accessory, trace the chart, confirm understanding by having them point to key process points as you describe them. Interaction increases their level of comfort, helps them take ownership, and builds value.

Verify

This is where you verify all the things you already know as they relate to the products and services you are presenting. Were you listening earlier? Did you take mental or physical notes? Now is the time to show off that beautiful memory and prove you were listening. "If I recall correctly, your biggest disappointment in your current dishwasher is the dishes aren't completely dry at the end of the cycle. I can imagine with a family of five, it must be frustrating and time-consuming to have to dry all those dishes by hand. The dishwasher I'm recommending performs extremely well in that area, let me show you what the manufacturer's done to solve that problem."

Engage

Ask before you tell! As you move from feature to feature, be sure to ask them a question before you tell them about it. Your question should be designed to lead to the features you want to discuss. When you ask a question, they respond. Based on their response, you tailor your feature benefit discussion to their response. As you move on to the next feature, you ask another question. BINGO! You've just avoided the product dump.

Instead of a one-sided boring and meaningless stream of information, you engaged in a two-way, meaningful conversation surrounding the features and benefits of your products and services. What problems have they had in the past related to what you are about to say? What desires will be satisfied with the features you are about to describe? These are the questions you will ask.

"Have you ever burned anything in a toaster?"

"Tons of times."

"Usually, that happens due to something getting jammed or settings that don't hold their accuracy. This toaster..."

Followed later by:

"Ever tried to put something in your toaster that was just too big?"

"Sure have, didn't work out well."

"Take a look at the slot sizes. Here, I have a few large items you can try yourself."

The possibilities are endless. Here are some additional examples:
- "Have you ever had to deal with a clogged toilet?"
- "Have you dealt with any previous liability due to a data breach?"
- "Are you familiar with the acoustic benefits of rosewood?"
- "What were you feeling the last time you had to really slam on your brakes?"

- "What percentage of your patients have presented with this side effect?"
- "Are you familiar with the way a court trial progresses?"
- "How much time and money do you spend each year to outsource that?"
- "Do you know why some paint jobs peel and flake?"
- "Would you like your insurance policy to be worth something while you're still living?"
- "Are you familiar with the benefits of setting it up as a Limited Liability Company rather than a full C Corporation?"

LIVE Your Product! Listen actively during your entire conversation and capture all of the information and data you will need during your product presentation. Use this information to properly verify that you are on the right track with your product and service recommendations. Engage your customer in an interactive conversation and demonstration by asking excellent questions; and please, avoid the product dump by all means necessary.

Key Takeaways – Chapter Eight

- LIVE Your Product: Listen, Interact, Verify, Engage.
- Focus on your customer's priorities as you actively give your presentation.
- The presentation of your products and services should be conversational, interactive and engaging.
- Engage your customer in the conversation by asking questions to reveal the importance and relevance of each feature and benefit.

CHAPTER NINE
NAVIGATE PRICE

"The truth is someone out there always has a better price. Someone out there always has bells and whistles you don't. The only thing that someone out there doesn't have is you."

NAVIGATE PRICE

  **NEVER**
Never pause at price.

  **ALWAYS**
Always focus on solving the problem and satisfying the desire.

  **VALIDATION**
Validation and Justification are more powerful than discounts, coupons and programs.

 INQUIRIES
Inquiries about the price should not be treated as objections to the price.

GIVE
Give your customer credit for their personal value system instead of imposing your own.

 **ADVOCATE**
Advocate for the customer if you absolutely have to lower the price.

 TAKE
Take something away if the objection is purely budgetary.

ENTHUSIASM
Enthusiasm passion and energy have landed infinitely more sales than price.

UNDERSTANDING PRICE

If you've related to your customer; guided them through your sales process correctly; elevated their experience; given them excellent advice; and provided an interactive and engaging product presentation, price should be less of an issue. In spite of all our efforts, however, sometimes price becomes central to the customer's decision process.

In this chapter, I will provide you with strategies to overcome the issue of price with your customers. I will not spend any time on overall pricing strategies or price positioning in your market. My focus will be on when and how you should introduce the price as well as some of the most common pitfalls sales professionals succumb to as they deal with price. I also discuss strategies that I believe work in all industries when dealing with price concerns and objections.

Change is a constant in the many industries I've worked with, and the way we help our customers navigate pricing is no exception. In most cases, I don't recommend handling price the same way today as I did 20 years ago. What's changed? In a nutshell, margin compression, increased competition, and the availability of information. Margins are smaller than they used to be; the ability to compare products and prices among competitors is easier than ever; in general, there are more comparable competitors than in the past. For these reasons, the difference in price among competitors (in most industries) is much less than it used to be. Why is this important? Because the price is no longer as important as it used to be. If you and I are competing for the same customer, have comparable products, and our prices are incredibly similar, what will our customers base their decision on? The answer to that question could be many things, but it probably won't be price. When the most differentiating factor is price, there must be offsetting factors that justify this difference.

Before the internet made product and price comparison information readily available, it was very time consuming to compare prices among competitors. Besides, margins were much higher. When it's challenging to compare competitors in an environment with sizable margins, price variation among competitors can be substantial. The same toaster might have been $20, $30, or $40 at different vendors. The same car at two different dealerships might have been $24,000 and $29,000. When price differences are substantial, it becomes the most significant differentiating factor. If an automotive customer faces a choice between saving $5,000 or getting a better experience elsewhere, they will pocket the money and deal with the bad experience. I've never heard anyone say, "I had to spend $29,000 instead of $24,000, but the experience was great." This is, of course, variable depending on the overall purchase price. For example, a $5,000 difference is much more significant on a $25,000 purchase than it is on a $500,000 purchase.

When price is highly differentiated, it's a good sales strategy to defer price conversations to the very final moments of the transaction (after we've had a chance to build more value). When price is marginally differentiated, we can be more transparent with pricing because it isn't significantly different than our competitors. The problem I see regularly is sales teams have not yet adapted to this new reality, and customers are unaware this new reality exists. Our customers still have the mindset that prices are highly differentiated, and traditional sales behavior supports that idea. They want to know the price right away to weed out competitors, and we are doing everything we can to hide it from them.

This is where a high degree of animosity blooms, and the adversarial nature of sales thrives. This calls for a higher level of transparency concerning the price as well as the need to be transparent about the reality of the marketplace. "This one's on sale for $32. Ten years ago, you might find a $10 to $15 difference if you were shopping around for a toaster. Today, all of us are priced within a couple of dollars of each other. Did you say you had four kids at home? This four-slice will be perfect."

Price and Value

Price is always in relation to value, and there is much more to value creation than the product or service itself. Value creation is part of all stages of the process, including consideration, comparison, shopping, transaction, acquisition, and ownership. Think back to all of the concepts we've covered in this book up to this point. If we have reframed our role as helping versus selling; used R7 effectively as an experiential consultant; intentionally guided our customers through the sales process efficiently; related to our customers on a human level; and elevated their experience, have we created enough value to justify our price? In essence, we, the sales professionals, are one of the most significant factors affecting value creation.

When I work with sales teams, there is inevitably at least one team member who blames their lack of success on the competition. "Their products are better than ours," or, "Their prices are more competitive." I've even worked with competitors that blame each other, with both groups telling me the other, "has more competitive pricing." ***The truth is someone out there always has a better price. Someone out there always has bells and whistles you don't. The only thing that someone out there doesn't have is you.*** If you are blaming the price or the product for your failure then you have to give the price and the product credit for your success, and if the price and the product are responsible for your sales success, *we don't need you!*

As you follow the strategies, tactics, and behaviors outlined in this book, value will increase, and price sensitivity will decrease. Having worked with and interacted with talented sales professionals all over the world in multiple industries, I've come to realize that those best at dealing with price all practice by a standard set of rules. I've packaged them for you in the following pages.

NAVIGATE PRICE

What would a model be without an acronym? NAVIGATE Price is more a set of rules than it is a model, but I wanted to make the rules easier to remember, so here they are:

1. **Never** pause at price.
2. **Always** focus on solving the problem and satisfying the desire.
3. **Validation** and justification are more powerful than discounts, coupons, and programs.
4. **Inquiries** about the price are not objections to the price.
5. **Give** the customer credit for their own value system.
6. **Advocate** for the customer if you absolutely have to lower the price.
7. **Take** something away if the objection is purely budgetary.
8. **Enthusiasm**, passion, and energy have landed exponentially more sales than price.

Full disclosure; all of the products and prices used in the following examples are real items available for sale today. I intentionally went looking for the highest-priced items I could find. I did this to point out that price isn't the most important factor to most people.

1. Never pause at price

Have you ever heard that you have to give your prospective customer the price and then go silent? "The first person to speak loses!" Haha. Don't do that. When we pause at price, we create a "decision point" for the customer. Unless price is the reason to purchase your product or service, you don't want to do that. Many salespeople have been conditioned to pause because this is where they expect an objection from their customer. They pause in anticipation of an objection. Don't do it! I'm not telling you not to pause at some point, just don't pause at price! Instead, give them the price without hesitation and then keep going until you either need to ask another question (**Research**), or give advice (**Recommendation**). A question will continue the conversation away from price, and a **Recommendation** will create a decision point. Here are three options to consider (two of them are acceptable):

- "The total price of these particular skis is $7,100."
- "The total price of these particular skis is $7,100. As we discussed, the core is solid granite, and the exterior is carbon fiber. We custom build every order, how soon do you need them?"
- "The total price of these particular skis is $7,100. Since you mentioned fit and style are important to you, I highly recommend the matching bindings so you can be confident they go together perfectly."

2. Always focus on solving the problem and satisfying the desire

Don't lose your focus and get caught up in a battle over the price. As price begins to become a significant issue in the conversation, make an effort to continue working toward the solution of the problem or the satisfaction of the desire. Remind your customer of all the benefits of following your recommendations. Ask questions that continue to move things forward toward a happy resolution. This is the perfect time to READ your customer.

What are they comparing as they evaluate your price? If their comparison is an exact duplicate, focus on everything you are providing *outside* the product as it relates to their situation. Will the transaction be more straightforward and less time consuming with you? Will their ownership experience be better as a result of working with you and your organization? Confirm and verify the customer's choices and show them how your product, solution, or recommended course of action meets their needs and desires better than the alternatives. PREACH luxury and make it easy for them to move forward.

3. Validation and justification are more powerful than discounts, coupons, and programs

In addition to the value we create as sales professionals, we should be aware of the inherent value in the choice the customer is making. In a search today on Google, I found a full-size mountain bike for $124. I found another one for $32,000. The moment someone decides to choose anything over the least expensive option, they are saying that there is more to this purchase than meets the eye. Is someone considering a $32,000 mountain bike looking for a discount, or are they looking for the validation and justification to pull the trigger? When someone balks at price, resist the urge to immediately move to a less expensive product or start offering discounts.

There is a reason they are choosing to spend more than the bare minimum, and they want to justify and validate that reason more than they want a discount. They deserve it. They've earned it. They will love it. Assuming that your recommendation is a good one, your role here is to help them remove doubt and make the right choice. Once you begin to lower the price, it often becomes a race to the bottom. There was a price. Now there is a lower price. Can it get lower? When you validate, you are effectively saying, "It's worth it." When you discount, you are effectively saying, "It's not worth it; let's try again."

In addition, especially pertaining to luxury brands, the customer is making a "worth it" statement of their own by purchasing. They are saying, "I'm worth it. I deserve it." When you go to a discount without first using validation and justification, you are telling your customer they aren't worth it and they don't deserve it.

4. Inquiries about the price are not objections to the price

What percentage of our customers are going to ask, "How much?" at some point in the conversation? If you have had the same experience as the vast majority of sales professionals I've worked with, you probably just said, "All of them." They are all going to inquire about the price, but that doesn't mean they are objecting to the price. "How much is it?" is not the same as, "Wow, I wasn't expecting that. I can get it for much less elsewhere." So, what's my advice? Don't treat a question about the price as if it were an objection to the price; just answer the question and move on. Remember rule #1: never pause at price! Remain calm. Once you answer the question, continue moving forward through R7. "This wallet is just over $800. Are antitheft and privacy important to you?"

5. Give the customer credit for their own value system

One of the biggest mistakes made regularly by salespeople is, metaphorically speaking, putting their shoes on their customers and forcing them to walk around in them. You are not your customer. Your role as a sales professional is to help your customers achieve their goals according to their value system, without judgment.

One of my clients recently updated one of their flagship products, and sales results were mixed; some salespeople sold more, some sold less, and some remained the same. I asked the sales team members individually, "What do you think of the update?" Some liked it, some didn't like it, and some were neutral. Can you guess which group they were in? Yes! A direct correlation.

This is a clear example of sales professionals imposing their own value system on their customers. The solution is to be enthusiastic about your customer's enthusiasm. If you are asked for your opinion directly, give it tastefully. "I can certainly see someone with your sense of style enjoying this keychain tremendously. It's only $3,200. Which keys are you going to keep on it?" Shopping around on the internet for fun, I found a pencil for $12,800, a dessert fork for $445, a t-shirt for $400,000, and a laptop for over $3,000,000. I wouldn't buy any of these, but I could sell them all and have a bunch of fun doing it. Seriously, don't you want to have a conversation with someone genuinely interested in buying a $400,000 t-shirt? I certainly would, "Where's the first place you're going to wear it?"

6. Advocate for your customers if you absolutely have to lower the price

If you have already given the customer your "best price" and, for competitive reasons, you absolutely have to lower it further, advocate for your customer. Go to bat for them, make a deal with your boss, find a program, take another look through the entire package, and dig deep for a way to shave some costs. Invoke your "price match guarantee." If you don't have one of those, go convince your sales manager to do it under this one circumstance. Review your records. What was your cost on the item? How long has it been in inventory? When you introduce the price change, tell your customer everything you did to bring the price down. You must have a reason for your ability to drop the price. Under no circumstances can you lower the price just because you could. This is the surest way to destroy your credibility and damage the customer's trust in you:

> "Wow, $30,000 is a little more than I wanted to spend on these sunglasses. I saw them at your competitor for only $28,000."
>
> "No problem, I can do that for you, shall I wrap them up?"
>
> "If you could do that for me, why didn't you do it already? If I had said they were $26,000, could you do that too?"

7. Take something away if the objection is purely budgetary

When your customer voices a true objection that is not competitive or comparison-based, it is usually budgetary. They aren't telling you someone else is cheaper or better; they are objecting because they simply want to pay less or realistically can't afford it. If I send one of my sons to the movies with a ticket and $5 for snacks, he can get a small popcorn or a bag of M&Ms, but not both. Can you picture the conversation?

> "Popcorn and M&Ms, that will be $10."
>
> "But I only have $5."
>
> "Well, you can get the popcorn or the M&Ms, but not both."

This doesn't mean my son doesn't want the popcorn and the M&Ms. It also doesn't mean he thinks the price is unfair. He's not suggesting that he could get a better price at another movie theatre, and he's not indicating that the popcorn and M&Ms here are inferior to anywhere else. He wants $10 worth of merchandise, and he only has $5 to spend. We are often in the same situation with our customers. When I asked a landscape/hardscape company to do an estimate for our property, he came back with an estimate of over $50,000. I told him I was thinking more in the $15,000 range. He said, "No problem, here's what we can do for $15,000 that will set us up to add things down the road."

When you are in this situation, have your customer prioritize. Remove pieces and options from the package; scale down your services; show them they can begin their dreams for what they have to spend now, and build on them into the future as they are able.

8. Enthusiasm, passion, and energy have landed exponentially more sales than price

When we combine skill, talent, and strategy with enthusiasm, passion, and energy, we go a long way toward defeating price issues. When products and services are being sold based on price, there is not a lot of added value in other areas. In sales situations, I'm a giant proponent of the idea that spending money should mean having a good time. The best sales professionals enjoy working with their customers; involve themselves in the outcome; express enthusiasm and passion for solving the problem, or satisfying the desire; and bring all their energy to the task. When this occurs, the issue of price gets smaller and smaller.

Before we Move On

This is the end of Part Two. You've now been introduced to all of the consultative models in this book. R7, STEP, PREACH, READ, LIVE and NAVIGATE. Don't stress if you can't keep them all straight just yet, as you continue they will eventually all come together into a cohesive framework. In Part Three, Chapters 10 through 14, we will revisit each of the Seven Rs in greater detail and begin weaving in the elements from the additional concepts I've presented.

Key Takeaways – Chapter Nine

- NAVIGATE Price.
- Price is no longer the most significant differentiating factor. You are.
- The more value you create through a positive experience, the less sensitive your customer will be to price.
- Transparency is your friend; don't make price an issue if it doesn't need to be.

PART THREE:

R7 STRATEGIES, EXPANDED

CHAPTER TEN
R1: RESEARCH REVISITED

*"We intentionally ask questions for a reason.
They are not random."*

THE POWER OF INQUIRY

Intentionality begins with inquiry. Without proactive **R**esearch, the sales profession is reduced to reacting to the customer's questions and providing information. In Chapter Four, I introduced **R**esearch as the first R in *The Seven Rs of Selling*. It's no mistake that **R**esearch comes first. Strategic questions are the key to mastering R7 and the accompanying models surrounding a consultative and experiential sales approach.

- Questions support our role as a professional consultant.
- Questions lead the conversation forward *proactively*.
- Questions solidify the topic of discussion, the direction of the conversation, and, ultimately, the destination.

- Questions create the "container" for our dialogue with our customers.
- Questions have *power*.

Just like any other power, questions may be used well or used poorly. An experienced sales professional has a "toolbox" full of questions. To achieve the desired outcome, you must use the correct tool, in the right way, at the appropriate moment. In the context of a sales conversation, there is a finite set of outcomes we are attempting to achieve. Therefore, we can craft a finite set of questions to help us succeed.

As you STEP Forward, PREACH Luxury, READ Your Customer, LIVE Your Product and NAVIGATE Price, questions will be your primary tools. Let's take a look at each of these and see how questions play a role:

STEP Forward
Strategic, Timely, Explicit, Purposeful

When we choose to embrace this model, we are deciding to be intentional about how we move through the sales process with our customers. We become proactive versus reactive. The alternative is to provide information solely in response to our customer's questions. Essentially, this is the difference between a sales professional and an information kiosk. When we STEP Forward, we assume the role of a guide. There are many paths we can take, so to head in the right direction we ask questions:

> *"You're interested in having us clean both the inside and the outside of the windows, correct?"*
>
> *"Yes."*
>
> *"And how many levels does the house have?"*
>
> *"Three."*
>
> *"Thank you. The next step will be to put a proper estimate together for you. To do that, we just need to do a quick exterior walk-around of the house. I don't want to surprise you at home, is there a convenient time tomorrow or Wednesday that will work best? I'll only need about 15 minutes."*

PREACH Luxury
Proactive, Real, Easy, Accommodating, Consistent, Human

The more we know about our customer's unique situation and the more understanding we have of the problem we are solving and the desire we are satisfying, the more proactive we can be to accomplish those goals. We know the most efficient route to get where the customer wants to go. By leading the conversation with questions, we make it easier for the customer. As we learn about our customers on a personal level, we can find ways to exceed their expectations, go above and beyond, and accommodate their unique needs. Being proactive, making things easy, accommodating specific circumstances, and connecting with our customer in a real and human way all begin with inquiry.

> *"I've got your insurance documentation ready to go. I just need your signatures. We can do it at my office, I can bring them out to you, or we can meet somewhere in between, what would work best?"*

READ Your Customer
Relate, Elevate, Advise, Discover

Relating, elevating, and advising all begin with discovery. The heart of this is **R**esearch. If we don't know anything personal about our customers, we have nothing to relate to. Having a positive conversation with our customers is so much easier to accomplish when we ask questions that are specifically designed to lead to a positive discussion. Giving advice and **R**ecommendations can't be done without a solid **R**eason and an emotional **R**eward. To discover these, we ask questions.

> *"What are you looking forward to most in your next home?"*

> *"Well, the kids are looking forward to having their own rooms, and we would love to have a gourmet kitchen. My wife and I love to cook together. A bigger garage would be a bonus, too."*

> *"I can relate, my husband would kill for a bigger garage."*

"Yeah, with all the kids' bikes and sports stuff, one of our cars is always in the driveway."

"Well, I'm fairly confident I can find all of those things for you. Has Charlotte always been home for you and your family?"

(Note: Can you see all the opportunities to relate? Take your pick: marriage, kids, cooking, garages, sports…)

LIVE Your Product
Listen, Interact, Verify, Engage

Before you listen, you must ask. The best way to avoid a boring one-way, "product dump" is to engage and involve your customer in a two-way conversation. You can't verify what you don't know. If you want your customers to interact with your products or materials, encourage them to do so with questions. I understand the need to give a robust presentation of features and benefits, but you must *ask before you tell!* Asking a strategic question increases the importance and relevance of what you are about to say to them.

> "Your husband told me you like to cook together. Do you also enjoy entertaining?
>
> The kitchen in this next home is perfect for that."
>
> "Here, hold this. It has great balance doesn't it? Now imagine being able to trim any of your trees and shrubs around your home without dragging a cord around.
>
> Batteries have come a long way, haven't they?"
>
> "Can you see how we've changed the landing page for your new website? Why don't you take the mouse?
>
> We want to make sure you're comfortable with the new navigation."
>
> "Are you familiar with the term "glamping?"

"You are absolutely going to love the interior of this RV."

"Have you ever worked with a contractor that didn't complete the job when they said they would?

Let me tell you about our project management team."

NAVIGATE Price

The ways in which questions help us navigate price are endless. Instead of pausing at price, we ask a question to steer the conversation in a positive direction. "This one's only $82,000, and it has the room to sleep your whole family. Have you decided where your first trip will be?"

As we focus on the customer's problem or desire, we ask questions that allow us to customize our **R**ecommendations and solidify our product or solution as the right choice. "The interest rate would be 5.75%. With the added elimination of your Private Mortgage Insurance, your payment will be reduced by more than $300 per month. Are you also interested in paying your mortgage off sooner? I could work up some options for you so you can see what those look like."

When a customer voices an objection, a question will help them justify and validate their decision as opposed to a statement, which usually comes across as defensive. "It looks like the one your comparing this too is a bit less expensive. Are you familiar with the extended five-year warranty offered on our product?" Instead of, "Yes, but ours has a five-year warranty, and theirs is only two."

When a customer inquires about the price (as opposed to an objection), we ask a question to move the conversation forward and focus on value creation. The alternative is to defend a price that didn't need defending, or offer a discount when it's not necessary. "We can manage your entire social media profile and online reputation for $1,800 per month. Are you focused more on generating business leads or your public relations messaging?"

Instead of imposing your value system on your customer, ask questions to help their value system come to life. "This refrigerator is just over $11,000. Don't you like how it will blend in seamlessly with your cabinetry?"

When we absolutely have to lower our price for competitive reasons, we use questions to prove our advocacy and verify the customer's commitment. "We don't have a price match guarantee, but I'd like to save you the trouble of going across town just to start over with someone else. Can you give me five minutes to see what I can do to make this happen for you?"

If the objection is budgetary, we use questions to prioritize and narrow down our product offering or solution recommendation. "While I'm convinced that she'd love both the necklace and the bracelet, which one do you think your daughter would prefer to have first?" Or, "If you're not ready for our full range of accounting services, we could start with the basics. What's consuming your time or causing you the most pain right now?"

Lastly, we may choose to ask questions that evoke enthusiasm, passion, and energy. "I got so excited about planning your vacation that I spent last evening looking at all of the available excursions. Did you see the half-day hike to the waterfall? That one might be my favorite."

EFFECTIVE QUESTIONS

As you can see, questions are imperative to the consultative sales process, but not all questions are created equal. We have to use the right tool for the job, and we have to use it in the right way. The first thing to understand when we are following R7 is that every question serves a purpose. ***We intentionally ask questions for a reason. They are not random.*** To review, we ask questions to:

- Gain insight and understanding so we can make appropriate **R**ecommendations.
- Learn about our customers and their situation to relate to them on a personal level and elevate their experience.
- Encourage our customers to interact and become engaged in our product presentation.
- Help our customers understand the full value of our offering.
- Intentionally move forward through the steps in the sales process.

Once we commit to using questions with purpose, we can set our minds to crafting the right questions and asking them in the right way at the right time. Remember, questions create a "container" for the conversation. Questions determine what we will talk about and where we are going next. The questions asked of us as human beings affect our thoughts, opinions, emotions, decisions, and actions. Within the confines of *The Seven Rs of Selling* I've grouped questions into four categories:

- Questions structured to gather information
- Questions structured to promote thought
- Questions structured to persuade and influence
- Questions structured to force or confirm a choice

Common to these four categories are two types of questions:

Closed Questions
- Offer minimal options to respond, often "yes" or "no."
- Are easier to answer.
- Create more predictable responses.
- Are more interrogative.
- Speed things up.

Open Questions
- Begin with "what," "why," "how," "tell me…"
- Prompt a more free-flowing wide range of responses.
- Gather more information
- Are more conversational
- Slow things down

As we follow the R7 methodology, we move fluidly through the Seven Rs. As we discover, we are conducting **R**esearch, building **R**apport, and identifying **R**easons for future **R**ecommendations. As we move to direction, we are stating and confirming **R**easons, offering **R**ecommendations, and explaining **R**ewards. During this process, we will consciously choose our questions based on what we are trying to accomplish. Are we gathering information, promoting thought, exerting influence, or forcing and confirming choices? We then formulate the question as open or closed based on whether or not we want to limit choices, where we want to go next in the conversation, and how quickly we want to get there. As we listen to the customer's responses, we are actively seizing on all opportunities to relate, elevate, and advise.

As you begin building your toolbox of questions, you will want to pay special attention to how you finish your question. If there is a "bad" response to your question, you are asking it in the wrong way. The simplest version of this is a "yes" or "no" question posed to the customer where a "no," response shuts down the sales process. Here are some examples:

- "Would you like to come and see it in person?" "NO"
- "Can I assume we are moving forward?" "NO"
- "Do you want to make an appointment?" "NO"
- "Are you ready to do this?" "NO"
- "Do you want to buy it or not?" Haha! "NO"

In most of these cases, you should replace your question with a **R**ecommendation. Now let's have another look at the four categories of questions with some examples.

Questions structured to gather information

Questions structured to gather information contain no steering, judgment, or confrontation. These questions are most commonly open, but can also be closed depending on the situation. Information gathering questions are useful when we are getting to know our customers and their overall situation. These questions can also be used to "check-in" with your customers about their experience with you.

Open Examples

"Tell me about your project." "What are you looking forward to when this is complete?" "What are you hoping to accomplish with me today?" "How soon are you hoping to complete this?" "What brings you in today?" "Why did you choose this particular brand?" "How am I doing with this so far?"

Closed Examples

"Are you considering a modern or traditional style?" "Is this part of a larger project?" "Are you planning to pick it up, or would you prefer we deliver it?" "Is this time-sensitive?" "Is this for a special occasion?" "Am I getting this right for you?"

Questions structured to promote thought:

Questions structured to promote thought are similar to information-gathering questions. However, they have the added element of steering and influencing the customer's pattern of thought. These questions are meant to help "paint the picture" of either the problem or the solution.

Open Examples

"What styles have caught your eye?" "What was your last move like?" "What would you change about the one you have now?" "How was your last experience purchasing X?" "Why now?" "How do you think he/she will react when you bring it home?"

Closed Examples

"Aren't you excited to feel that Mediterranean sun on your face?" "Have you ever broken or lost your phone?" "Have you ever been in an accident?" "Which one is he/she going to kiss you for?"

Questions structured to persuade and influence:

Questions structured to persuade and influence are directional and assuming. You should use these questions with a bit of caution. If they are used too early without reason, they come across as aggressive. When you want to be more forceful, use a **R**ecommendation instead of a question.

Open Examples

"How do you want it packaged?" "What accessories are you considering to go with that?" "Now that we've selected the sofa, can you tell me what you are thinking for armchairs?" "What are you considering for your

next project?" "What other marketing channels do you want to pursue?"

Closed Examples

"With the addition of the children, are you ready to beef up your life insurance?" "Have you considered refinancing to lower your payment?" "You don't want to pass up on the matching scarf, do you?" "Would a weekday or Saturday be a more convenient time for you?" "Why don't we write it all up for you so you can make a final decision?"

Questions structured to force or confirm a choice

Questions structured to force or confirm a choice are frequently used when it's time to move forward in the sales process. Indecision can freeze the sales process. These are the kinds of questions that finalize decisions and continue progress. When we ask a question with infinite possible responses, we paralyze our customers with indecision.

Instead of, "When would be a good time?" we ask, "Would Tuesday or Wednesday be better?" Rather than trying to pick a perfect time (which doesn't usually exist), they are "forced" to choose the most acceptable alternative. These are often used just prior to or just following a Recommendation.

Open Examples

"How are we doing with the final color selection?" "What consideration have you given to the settlement offer?" "Why don't we narrow down the style, and then we can tackle the size?" "We've got the size locked in, which patterns appeal to you?"

Closed Examples

"So, we're set on the silver handles?" "It has to be completed by the 6th, is that correct?" "You definitely want the quarterly cleaning package?" "So, you're available on the 22nd for us to start?" "You're set with the two shirts, right? Let me help you pick a couple of matching ties; would you prefer solid colors or patterns?"

Summary

Mastering the art of asking questions is an essential skill set. As you hone your skills in this area, consider what you are trying to accomplish, how you want to move forward, and where you want to guide your customer next. Correctly phrase your questions to "contain" the possible responses. Just like every courtroom drama you've ever seen, if you're not prepared for the answer, don't ask the question.

NESTED QUESTIONS

As your repertoire of strategic questions grows, and you identify common patterns of behavior in your customers, you will begin to see a specific series of questions working in tandem. You've heard me describe questions as creating a "container" for the conversation. As you string questions together in context, your container will grow exponentially. Soon you will uncover a particular question which, when asked, leads to a predictable outcome. This is due to the way the questions fit together in a structure. The customer's response to your first question leads to your next question. I call these nested questions. When you ask this series of questions correctly, there are no possible responses to your questions which fall outside of the container you've created. If you've ever seen nesting dolls, you get the picture. Once you open the first one, they all lead to the center. Nested questions are like this, too, questions within questions. Here's an example to illustrate the point:

Veronica the kitchen designer

Veronica has been a kitchen designer for many years. As she has honed her skills, she has become a master at asking questions as a way to guide her prospective customers through the design process. She also realizes the value of **R**apport, and has become quite good at sharing her own personal details when appropriate. Veronica has even begun to intentionally structure her questions to move in that direction. She's just answered a call from Grace, who is interested in remodeling her kitchen. They've been talking for only a minute or two and have exchanged pleasantries.

Veronica wants to move forward in the process, so she asks one of her favorite questions:

"Tell me about your project, Grace."

"Well, we started with the idea of replacing our cabinets and countertops, but if our budget allows, we're looking to redo our kitchen completely. We're even looking at adding a window on one side and removing a wall."

"So, you went from a makeover to a do-over. Do you have an idea of when you would like to have it fully completed?"

"We're usually the hub for our family's holiday party, so we'd definitely like to be done by early December at the latest."

"Sounds fun, we usually go to my brother's. I have two kids, but he has five. It's way easier for us to go to him."

"Five kids! Wow. We have two as well, but they're grown now."

"Your timeline is tight but achievable. Where in town is your project located?"

"We're in South Park, on Delaney."

"I know that area well, I've designed a few kitchens down there. Grace, have you considered what style of kitchen you are considering: modern, traditional, contemporary?"

"Well, I have some pictures and magazines that I like, but it seems like a bit of a mix. Contemporary, I guess."

"And have you spoken with a general contractor?"

"No, we haven't."

"OK, perfect. Here's what I'd like to do. I want to do this right, so let's set up a time for me to come and see your space. You can show me exactly what you're planning. I'll show you my portfolio, and with the pictures *and magazines you have, we'll design something beautiful. With your permission, I'm also going to bring a general contractor that I work with quite a bit. When we start moving walls and adding windows, I want to be sure everything is perfect. If we're going to get this done in time for your family's holiday, we shouldn't waste any time. Would Monday or Tuesday work better for you this coming week?"*

While this conversation sounded natural, Veronica was employing a tremendous amount of skill and strategy. Veronica always leads in with four basic questions: project, timeframe, location, and style. Veronica knows she will ask these questions in sequence. Let's look at these from Veronica's point of view:

Project

"Tell me about your project?" is Veronica's favorite question. This very open, information-gathering question gives her a foundation to work with for the rest of the conversation. Not only does she usually learn all about the project itself, but also about the customer. Even though this is an open question, Veronica has "closed" it mentally by categorizing all possible responses. In Veronica's mind, there are only three possibilities: makeover, do-over, and demolition. A makeover happens more rapidly. A do-over is Veronica's favorite kind of project, as it allows her more creativity and is usually more profitable. A demolition will take the most time. With both a do-over and a demo she will involve a general contractor if the customer doesn't already have one.

Timeframe

Once she has an understanding of the overall project, the next question is, "Do you have an idea of when you would like to have it fully completed?" In her mind, there are only three possible responses: enough time, plenty of time, and not enough time. Later in the conversation, this will inform her **R**ecommendation. With enough time, it becomes a **R**eason to meet right away and get started. With plenty of time, she would reword her **R**ecommendation. "It's fortunate we have so much time, most people wait until it's stressful. This way, we can take our time and get the design perfect without having to stress or worry about it." When there is not enough time, this creates urgency as well, but also the need to explain this reality to the customer and reset expectations.

Location

"Where in town is your project located?" is Veronica's third question. She's categorized possible responses as: somewhere she's done work before and somewhere she hasn't. If she has, she will mention it. If she has not, she will rephrase her response. "I know that area, I've designed several kitchens nearby." By this point in the conversation, she knows whether or not she will recommend meeting at the customer's home. To provide date and time options for the customer, she needs to know where she will be going.

Style

"Have you considered what style…?" is usually Veronica's final question before moving on to her **R**ecommendation. She has categorized her customer's responses into only two categories: sure about the style and not sure about the style. Based on this, Veronica will phrase her **R**ecommendation appropriately. This question also allows her to show off her expertise and build her credibility. Regardless of how the customer responds, she will be mentioning her portfolio.

"Have you spoken to a general contractor?" was added due to the wall and the window. The addition of the contractor in the **R**ecommendation is a way to elevate the customer's experience and make everything easier down the road. Veronica has learned through repeated conversations that these four questions in tandem are an excellent combination, providing her the opportunity to relate, elevate, and advise. Her final question wasn't, "Will Monday or Tuesday work for you?" which is a "yes" or "no" question. Veronica was forcing a choice by asking, "Would Monday or Tuesday work better…?" Veronica would have used this same sequence of questions if someone walked into her studio or sent her an email asking about her services.

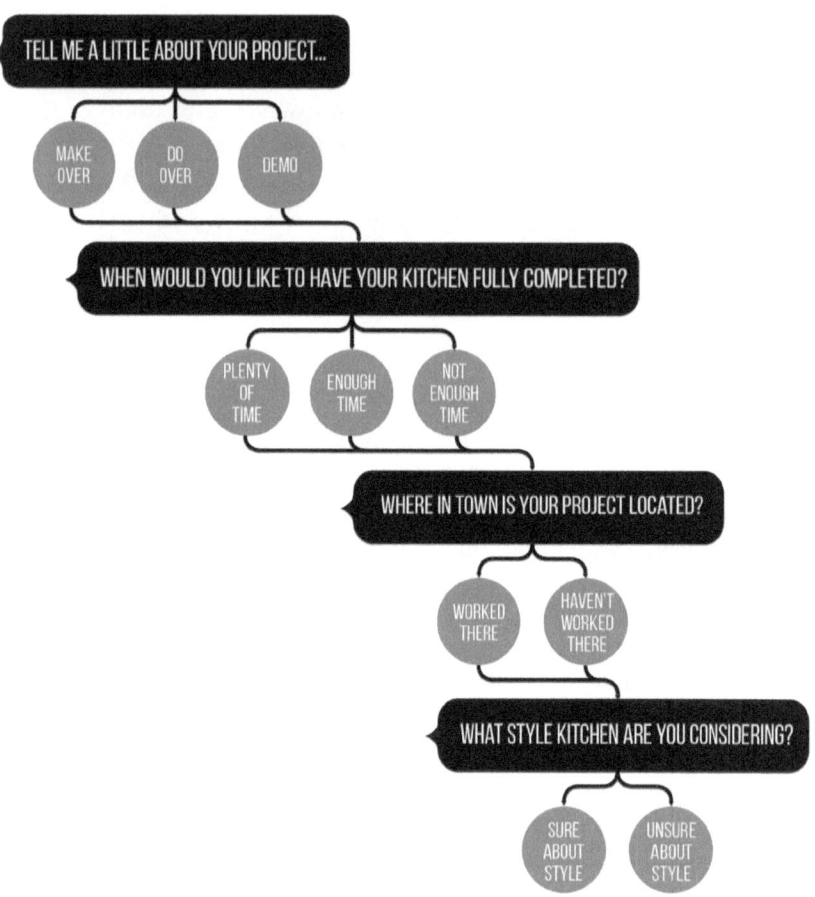

When she meets with her customers at their home, she will begin another series of nested questions. "Show me what you had in mind." "Tell me how you entertain?" and "How do you typically prepare meals; what kind of cooking do you do?" This series of nested questions will give her all the information she will need to make excellent **R**ecommendations as well as continue to relate and elevate.

Once created, a series of nested questions is extremely powerful and easy to use. The most challenging part is to be sure you have a course of action in mind for every possible response you might receive. This is what creates the "container." You must categorize all of the possible responses to each of your questions, as Veronica has done above.

Nested questions may also be used to steer your customer to an inevitable conclusion. As an example, I often conduct workshops with groups of very successful and experienced sales professionals. At the beginning of the session, I want everyone to be open to learning new methods and exploring my ideas. Could you imagine if I simply asked, "How many of you are open to learning new methods and exploring my ideas today?" I'm fairly sure I'd hear crickets. I know the sales environment is changing. I know learning new methods and adapting will be essential for success. I could just tell them, "The sales environment is changing. Learning new methods and being open to new ideas will help you continue to succeed in the future." But it would be so much more powerful if this understanding came from them instead of me. So, I ask this series of questions:

- Has the environment you are selling in changed at all in the past 20 years?
- If you were still selling the same way you were 20 years ago, would you be as successful as you are?
- Do you believe things are going to change over the next 10 years?
- If we don't adapt to those changing circumstances, how successful will we be?
- How many of you are open to learning new methods and exploring my ideas today?

They would all agree that the environment has changed drastically. They would admit that they would not have been successful without adapting to these changes. They would agree that things are going to change, and new skills and ideas will be required to be successful. At the end, when I ask my final question, they will all raise their hands. The VP at one of my larger clients calls this a "Jedi mind trick." As long as your intentions are pure and the outcome is positive for your customer, this is an excellent way to move forward in a sales process, reach an inevitable conclusion, or gain the ability to make a specific **R**ecommendation. I'll explore this more when we revisit **R**easons, **R**ecommendations, and **R**ewards in Chapter 12.

When you structure a series of nested questions and mentally control the possible responses with categories, you create a "container" in which relating, elevating, and advising become automatic and consistent. Our ability to influence and persuade is tremendously enhanced when we've built a comprehensive set of questions, and we understand how to flow through them. Using your **Research** expertise to understand your customers and their situation will lead you to give excellent advice. Research is the foundation of R7.

> **Key Takeaways – Chapter 10**
>
> - Questions gather information, promote thought, persuade and influence, and force or confirm choices.
> - Questions put a container around your dialogue with the customer; they control topic, direction and destination.
> - Questions are the most powerful and versatile tools in a consultant's toolbox.

CHAPTER ELEVEN
R2: INTENTIONAL RAPPORT

*"Our customers want to like us,
they just don't expect to like us."*

A QUICK REVIEW OF RAPPORT

Remember, **R**apport is not interviewing, interrogating, or "fact-finding." It's a two-way exchange of information. People buy from people they like, but how will they like you if they don't know anything about you? What's shared by the sales professional is just as important as what is shared by the customer. We allow the customer to see a bit of our truth as it relates to their truth. What we share is always in relation to what they've shared with us.

We know and freely admit that there is a tremendous value for both parties when we relate to each other, and we understand the importance of building **R**apport early, and often. ***Our customers want to like us, they just don't expect to like us.*** However, they are hopeful; they don't enter a sales situation and say, "Boy, I really hope I get someone who's miserable, untrustworthy, and unhelpful." We are not going to convince our customers that all salespeople in the world are truly wonderful people, but we are going to allow them to see a little bit of our reality. In this way, we humanize ourselves and begin earning trust. The conversation and transaction becomes more relaxed, less stressful, and more enjoyable for both parties. Here's a quick review of **R**apport:

Rapport is

- Connecting, relating and sharing the human condition
- Genuine, real, human and true
- Intentional
- Simple and brief

Rapport is not

- An interview or an interrogation
- Uncomfortable or awkward
- Just about finding something in common
- All about you

While finding something in common can help establish **R**apport, so can finding nothing in common. I've come across salespeople that keep asking customers questions until they find something in common, often turning it into an awkward interrogation. "Do you like golf? No, fishing? Do you have a dog? Any kind of pet? Do you like wine? Are you breathing? You are? Wow, me too!"

If building **R**apport is something you want to do early, and often, you need a strategy to do so. You also need to clearly understand when it is beginning to take shape between you and your customers, even when your conversation is happening through different mediums, such as phone, email, or chat.

"THE MOMENT OF CONNECTION"

When did **R**apport begin between us? It turns out this is a relatively easy question to answer. After reviewing thousands of sales conversations through different channels, I've pinpointed the moment it happens. I call it "The Moment of Connection." It's not complicated, and it's pretty easy to identify. It occurs when the customer outwardly recognizes and expresses interest in the sales professional as another human being. They do this by commenting on, or asking a question about, the sales professional on a personal level. You've seen this many times in previous chapters, but here's another example:

> *"Scott told me you wanted to discuss a potential acquisition. Have you gone through this process before?"*
>
> *"No, this is the first time we've considered it. We know they are interested in selling, but it might be a bit delicate. We've been competitors for years, and they are a family-owned business just like us."*
>
> *"That is an interesting situation, but not unheard of. I went into law myself, but my family has a small business here in town as well. I know how interesting it can be."*
>
> *"It's never without its challenges. What kind of business is your family in?"*
>
> *"They do a lot of municipal snow-removal in the winter and…"*

That's it. "The Moment of Connection" happens when the customer comments on something personal about you, or asks a question about you personally. Something changes at this moment. Barriers come down, resistance diminishes, and the door opens to collaboration rather than conflict. I have witnessed, heard, or read this type of scenario play out in person, by phone, and through written exchange thousands of times. The positive difference in the conversation past this point is tangible and meaningful. In practice, this is a three-step process:

1. The customer shares something you can personally relate to.
2. You relate to that element of the conversation on a personal level.
3. The customer comments on, or poses a question, regarding what you've revealed.

When I analyzed the behaviors of the most successful salespeople, I inevitably found that this personal connection was occurring more consistently, more frequently, and earlier in the conversation. The big revelation, however, was the realization that the most successful individuals were sharing the same personal detail about themselves over and over again.

"THE STRATEGIC REVEAL"

This next revelation might come as a blow. Are you sitting down? Are you ready? OK, here goes, not everything about you is interesting. I know. I'm sorry. It's ok. Take a breath. I felt the same way. In all sincerity, the reality is that some things about us are more interesting than others. Some things about us are mundane, ordinary, plain, and even boring. On the other hand, some things about us are remarkable, memorable, and relatable. These things are the basis for "The Strategic Reveal."

When I spoke with the sales professionals who had consistent success with **R**apport, I asked them why they were sharing the same detail again and again. Their response? "It works!" It turns out, some things about us are more likely to generate a positive response than others. In retrospect, this wasn't all that surprising. What was astonishing, however, was the intentionality behind this. We can agree that sharing something about ourselves in relation to some personal detail about our customers is advantageous; whereas sharing something about ourselves disconnected from our customers is incongruous, out of context, and uncomfortable. When a customer says, "We've got two children and one on the way," then responding with, "I'm not quite there yet, I just got engaged," makes complete sense. Responding with, "I play guitar," would be somewhat ridiculous.

So, how was it that one of the more successful sales reps I spoke with was sharing, "I play guitar," with every customer? What was occurring that made this personal detail appropriate to every customer conversation? What I found was the addition of an additional step to the three-step process. It's actually the *first* step:

1. *Ask a question prompting the customer to share something connected to what you plan to share.*
2. The customer shares something you can personally relate to.
3. You relate to that element of the conversation on a personal level.
4. The customer comments on, or poses a question, regarding what you've revealed.

Once again, **R**esearch was the key. These sales professionals weren't waiting for something to happen in the conversation to produce **R**apport naturally. They were intentionally causing it to happen by asking a question, triggering their ability to share what they were *planning* to share. As a result, they encouraged a human connection more frequently, and much earlier in the process. Also, they weren't just sharing any old piece of information. They were sharing something they knew from experience would generate positive **R**apport. We labeled this method, "The Strategic Reveal," and we've been teaching it ever since.

To employ "The Strategic Reveal" and begin following the process above, you've got to get two things right. First, what is it about you that is interesting enough to be commonly appealing? Second, what question will you ask to lead to your "Strategic Reveal?"

At the time of this writing, I have four children. They are all boys. According to the U.S. Census, just over 8% of families in the U.S. have three or more children. I'm sure it's much lower for families that have four or more children. Adding to that, all four of mine are boys, making it all that much more uncommon. When I tell someone, "I've got four children, all boys," it almost always leads to positive rapport, which is why this is my go to "Strategic Reveal." The most common responses are something like:

- "Wow, that must be busy." (It is.)
- "Your wife must be a saint." (She is.)
- "Sounds crazy, are they involved in sports?" (They are.)

- "We've only got two. I can't imagine four!" (You get used to it.)
- "No wonder you travel so much for work." (Not true!)
- "I don't have any yet, wow!" (Take your time.)
- "Aren't you going to try for a girl?" (We did try. His name is Jack)

This reveal works well for me. Family is something everyone can relate to. We all have one, or we've been a part of one. Luckily for me, family is contextually relevant in most industries and human conversations. Appliances, vehicles, home sales, insurance, financial planning, and dozens more. Luckily for you, you can choose from a variety of excellent details. Here are a few examples:

Big life events

- Graduation
- Engagement
- Marriage
- Birth of child
- Buy a home or move
- Become an empty nester
- Big career change

Vacation / Recreation

- Past vacation or travel
- Future vacation or travel plans
- Hobbies
- Recreational activities

Location / Region

- I'm originally from _____
- I've grown up here all my life
- I've been there
- I've never been there
- I've always wanted to go there
- I don't know where that is

Whatever you choose to use, it must be relevant, humanizing, appropriate, and strategic. Your reveal must evoke a positive response from your customer in the vast majority of cases. If it's hit or miss, choose something else. Additionally, there is nothing in the rule book that requires you to have just one "Strategic Reveal." You can have as many as you want. The essential part is that you don't wait for **R**apport to happen naturally, or leave it up to chance.

Once you've landed on a personal detail that works well, the next step is to design a question. Your question must be within the context of a normal conversation and encourage the customer to share something personal. The question you ask should be engineered to discover something you can strategically relate to. In my case, it would depend on the industry. Here are some examples:

- **Insurance**
  - "I want to recommend the right kind of policy as well as the correct coverage amount; how large is your family?"
- **Real Estate**
  - "How many bedrooms are you looking for?"
- **Appliances**
  - "How many mouths are you feeding at home?"
- **Automotive**
  - "Will this vehicle primarily be for work or family?"
- **Furniture**
  - "Do you want a living room set that is more child-friendly?"

In all of the situations above, there is no possible response which would negate my ability to share that I have four children. When you design your question well, it works perfectly every time. In some cases, you may have to use a "nested question" to get all the way to your "Strategic Reveal." I worked with one gentleman who wanted to use, "I used to be on the Olympic shooting team," as his reveal. Asking his customers, "Do you like guns?" was out of the question. As he was in the world of appliances and kitchen cabinetry, he began by asking, "What kind of cooking do you enjoy? Do you like international food?" Regardless of their response, he could answer, "I've learned to like just about everything. I've traveled to

17 different countries." This would prompt his customers (a very high percentage of the time) to ask, "Were you in the military or something?" which allowed him to say, "no, I was on the Olympic shooting team." Get creative if you need to!

If, for some reason, you can't think of an interesting personal detail to use for this purpose, use location. Everyone is from somewhere. I have yet to find it awkward to ask, "So, has this area always been home for you?" in any given professional situation. This question is almost always answered in one of two ways, "Yes, I've been here all my life," or, "No, I'm originally from _____." Either way, your customer's reveal leads to your ability to share one of the following:

- I'm originally from _____
- I've grown up here all my life
- I've been there
- I've never been there
- I've always wanted to go there
- I don't know where that is

Regardless of what you choose, continue to refine your question and your reveal until it is as close to perfect as you can get. Once you hit on the right combination, you will see a pattern develop in your conversations, leading to **R**apport earlier, and more often.

Reveal / Conceal

My wife and I hosted a murder-mystery party at our home many years ago. There were four couples, and we had a blast. We all showed up in character and costumes. We played the game with rounds of conversation among the characters. None of us, even the eventual culprit, knew "whodunit." Each participant had a reveal/conceal card. During each round, we all asked each other questions and had a conversation. While everything on each card was true, not all of it was meant to be revealed. Certain things had to be entered into the conversation proactively (revealed), and certain things were meant to be hidden if possible (concealed). This is an excellent analogy for the sales process as it pertains to relating on a personal level with our customers. Some things are advantageous to reveal, and others are best concealed.

While building **R**apport is about connecting your truth with that of your customer, if your customer says, "I'm taking a big vacation to celebrate my divorce," now is not the time to say, "Oh yeah? I've been through six of those myself. What attorney did you use? Mine gave me a punch-card, my next one's half price." All joking aside, anything obviously inappropriate should be permanently etched on your conceal card. Less obviously, anything that draws concern, pity, sadness or anger should be concealed under most circumstances. We should conceal things like, "I'm sorry about the frog in my throat, I've been sick for a week, or, "I can't, I'm leaving early today. My kids are all sick at home." We want our customers to enjoy their experience, remember? Anger, sadness, pity, and concern are usually not pleasant emotions.

At an airport restaurant recently, I ordered a chicken and bacon wrap. After 15 minutes, the waitress came and asked me, "Is your plane leaving soon?" I replied that I had plenty of time, at which point, she said, "OK, my cook is out on another one of his marathon smoke breaks. If your plane was leaving soon, I could just make it myself." Um… no thank you? Now I have a choice of having my meal prepared by Smoky the Cook or Whiny the Waitress. I'll pass. That's a definite conceal. How about, "My cook will be back in a few minutes, but if you're pressed for time, I'd be happy to make it for you."

Lastly, anything detrimental to the sale, such as "I don't own that," or, "I've never used that brand," should probably be concealed. "It's been super slow here lately," and "We don't really sell very many of these," are likewise probably a bad idea. I'm not asking you to lie, just don't volunteer concealable items voluntarily. I'll never understand why the sales reps at my wireless carrier are always going out of their way to tell me they don't use the same brand of phone that I have (and paid a lot of money for). I didn't ask, and I don't want to know. Keep a tight rein on what you reveal and conceal. As you move forward into a longer-term relationship, you will be able to broaden your topics of discussion and the range of items you share.

Key Takeaways – Chapter 11

- **R**apport leads to trust, which is essential for any helping relationship.
- A true sales professional develops **R**apport intentionally, early, and often.
- Not everything about you is interesting. Some things should be revealed, some concealed. Choose wisely.

CHAPTER TWELVE
R3-R4-R5: RECOMMENDATION STATEMENTS

"Your advice will always have a much greater impact if you state the reasons the customer gave you, rather than those you may have assumed."

REASONS – RECOMMENDATIONS – REWARDS

In Chapter Four, I introduced the idea that **R**ecommendations are at the very center of the R7 strategy. The **R**ecommendation is where you cross over from sales into consulting and exercise your value as an advisor and guide. Providing advice and guidance is how we help people instead of sell stuff.

The discovery process ultimately leads to the ability to provide direction to our customers in the form of advice and guidance. We do this through a "Recommendation Statement," which combines R3, R4, and R5; **R**easons, **R**ecommendations, and **R**ewards. When we learned to STEP Forward, we discussed the importance of timing. If we have related to our customers on a human level and discovered substantial **R**easons to move forward, it is time to make our **R**ecommendation. If you have been READing Your Customer, you have also seized every opportunity to elevate their experience.

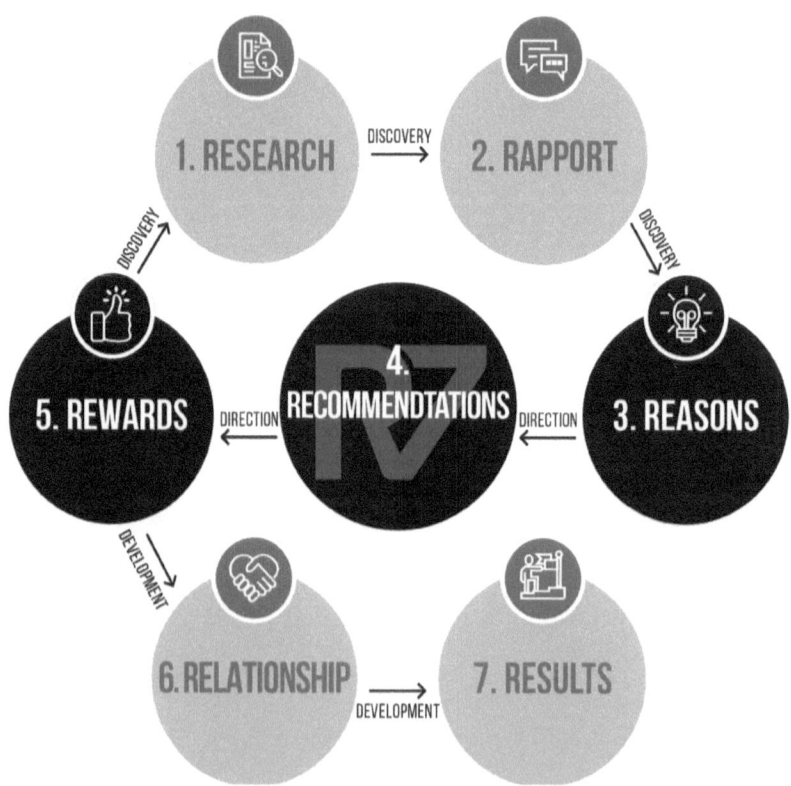

In this way, you are in the best possible position to move the sales process forward. At this moment in time, our client likes us, trusts us, and is having an enjoyable experience. When you give **R**easons for your **R**ecommendation and explain the emotional **R**ewards of following your advice, you build the most reliable foundation for success. A **R**ecommendation alone creates doubt and indecision and is often questioned. A **R**eason and a **R**ecommendation together are stronger, but lack emotional motivation. Some customers make decisions more logically, others more emotionally. Most people combine both logic and emotion when making decisions, which is why you should always provide both **R**easons and **R**ewards. Here is an example:

- "I recommend you plead guilty."
- "The evidence against you is overwhelming. I recommend you plead guilty."
- "The evidence against you is overwhelming. I recommend you plead guilty. Otherwise, you could spend the rest of your life in a super-max."

In the last example, we've avoided the questions, "Why are you recommending I plead guilty?" and, "What happens if I don't?" This last example is obviously the most compelling and the easiest to agree to. In this case, it's also what's best for the client, which all **R**ecommendations should most definitely be.

When we shift to direction with a "Recommendation Statement," we also change our voice and our attitude. We move from being "helpfully curious" to being more confident, reasonable, and educational. We assume the role of an expert, providing excellent guidance in a truthful and genuine way. Different industries and situations may call for a more concerned tone of voice, or possibly an authoritative demeanor. Your circumstances will dictate this shift.

In addition to our tone of voice, it is critical to consider our word choice. Words like maybe, possibly, or probably do not confer confidence. "Maybe you should try the new surgical alternative," says the doctor. "Maybe I should get a second opinion," says the patient. Instead of, "We can probably match that price," we say, "I will definitely do my best."

There is a particular phrase I believe you should staunchly avoid. In fact, please raise your right hand. Are you raising it? OK, repeat after me:

"I solemnly swear that I will never ever use the following three words in a sales situation ever again: LET ME KNOW."

When we say, "Let me know," we transfer leadership of the conversation over to the customer; we put them in charge of the next steps; and we voluntarily put ourselves in "wait and see" mode. If you clearly see the steps forward for your customers, and you are attempting to move in that direction, you don't want to say (or write) "let me know." When we are providing advice, we don't want to say:

- "Let me know when or if you want to proceed."
- "Let me know when you're ready."
- "Let me know when you've spoken with…"
- "Let me know if you have any more questions."

It's perfectly ok to say, "let me know," in a non-sales situation when there are no consequences to a decision. "Let me know if you prefer the black or silver trim," or "Let me know if you want to pick it up or have it delivered," are both acceptable. However, try to imagine a doctor saying, "Let me know when you're ready to take this medication," or a parent saying, "Let me know if you'd like to study for that big test." In both of these situations, we would expect directional advice and guidance. When there are logical next steps to take, which will benefit the customer, we replace, "let me know," with a **R**ecommendation.

- "To bring your blood pressure down, I'm recommending this particular medication."
- "You told me you were going to work hard to bring your grades up, so I'd suggest we get started by studying for that big test."

Your ability to provide solid direction, advice, and guidance using the right language at the right time and in the right tone will help you help your customers.

CRAFTING "RECOMMENDATION STATEMENTS"

When learning and implementing *The Seven Rs of Selling*, the "Recommendation Statement" is one of the most critical practical elements. It brings together the **Reason**, **Recommendation**, and **Reward** in one fluid combination. The "Recommendation Statement" moves the process forward, finalizes decisions with your customer, builds the overall solution, and eventually closes the sale. Throughout most sales processes, the **Recommendations** we make will be many and varied. We may be recommending a specific product or service. We may be recommending a particular model, accessory, upgrade, or add-on. We may be recommending a course of action or the movement from one step in the process to the next. We will repeatedly be cycling from R1 through R5.

Since it is likely we will be making multiple "Recommendation Statements" we should avoid saying, "Because of _____ I recommend _____ so you can _____," every time we make a Recommendation, which would get repetitive and impersonal very quickly. With this in mind, it's advantageous to learn and become comfortable with many different ways of stating **Reasons**, **Recommendations**, and **Rewards**. Let's isolate each element of the "Recommendation Statement" and review some alternative phrasing.

Reasons

Here are a some different ways to lead into the **Reasons** for your Recommendations:

1. "Because you mentioned _____, I recommend…"
2. "Based on _____, I recommend…"
3. "It sounds like _____, so I recommend…"
4. "Now that I understand _____, I would recommend…"
5. "With _____ in mind, I would recommend…"
6. "I'm actually excited that you _____, I'd recommend…"
7. "Since you (have, are, will, need, want…) _____, I would recommend…"

8. "As you (have, are, will, need, want…) _____, I would recommend…"
9. "Due to the fact that you _____, I recommend…"
10. "Keeping in mind that _____, I'd recommend…"
11. "In order to _____, I'd recommend…"
12. "After reviewing _____, I'd recommend…"

Recommendations

These are many ways of following your **Reasons** with a **Recommendation**, (I covered some of these in Chapter 4):

1. "Because of _____, I suggest you…"
2. "Because of _____, the next step for you would be to…"
3. "Because of _____, you should really consider…"
4. "Because of _____, the best course of action is…"
5. "Because of _____, let's do this first then…"
6. "Because of _____, here's what I'd like to do for you…"
7. "Because of _____, I'd encourage you to…"
8. "Because of _____, I would definitely look at…"
9. "Because of _____, the best thing to do would be to…"
10. "Because of _____, I believe _____ would be extremely helpful for you."
11. "If I were _____, I would definitely…"
12. "Most of my customers _____, so I'd advise you to…"

Rewards

Rewards typically follow the **Recommendation**, providing the emotional motivation for your customer to accept your advice. They explain the benefit of what they are going to get. **Rewards** either provide something positive or avoid something negative. Here are some examples:

1. "I recommend _____, so you can…"
2. "I recommend _____. This way, you will be able to…"

3. "I recommend _____, which will allow you to…"
4. "I recommend _____, to give you the ability to…"
5. "I recommend _____, in order to…"
6. "I recommend _____, to make sure that…"
7. "I recommend _____, to ensure that…"
8. "I recommend _____, because I want to make sure that…"
9. "I recommend _____. Otherwise, you'll have to…"
10. "I recommend _____, so you won't have to…"
11. "I recommend _____. This will avoid…"
12. "I recommend _____. I don't want you to…"

With the above alternatives in mind and some serious practice, you will have quite a few different ways of making a "Recommendation Statement." (For you math fans, there are more than 1700 combinations if you use the alternatives I've provided). With some effort, I'm convinced you could develop hundreds of your own. An essential element of this is to use language that's comfortable for you. I'm not trying to provide you with a "script," so much as I'm trying to ingrain the use of this strategy in your everyday conversations with customers. Let's take a look at a few examples:

- "Since your guests will have some downtime between the ceremony and the reception, I'd like to add the photo booth to your package. The booth will allow them to be occupied and engaged while you're getting photos taken, and it will create some wonderful memories for you. You said you wanted it to be fun and fast-paced, and this will definitely do that."
- "I'm glad you told me that you wanted this suit to stand out and get noticed. We can have a little fun with our design. I'd suggest we go with functioning buttons on the cuffs as well as a custom liner on the inside. We can even add contrast stitching to the buttonholes to give it that extra pop. You're going to love it!"
- "With the errands you have to run after this, let's do the VIP service so I can wash everything out. I can double-check everything and get any stray strands, and you won't be uncomfortable and itchy while you're running around."

To employ this strategy, we consider the alternative **R**ecommendations we might make with any given customer, and we use **R**esearch to get the **R**easons out in the open and make them explicit. Let's see how this might look in another example:

Justin the moving company representative

Justin is a sales representative for a moving company. He's been doing this professionally for a few years and has been moderately successful. He knows he could increase his overall sales, and he's identified packing and unpacking services as his most significant opportunity. His closing ratio for moving services is better than average compared to his peers. Still, the add-on of packing and unpacking services is slightly below the average. Justin made a list of all the benefits of these services so he could be better prepared to explain the value to his customers. This is what he came up with:

- Time savings
    - The customer won't have to pack and unpack themselves.
- Convenience
    - In just a day or two, everything will be in its place in the new residence. Unpacked boxes won't be all over the place.
- Less chance of damage to property
    - Boxes will be packed and unpacked by professionals with experience.
- Insurance
    - Justin's company will not insure what they do not pack and unpack themselves.

Armed with this information, Justin explained all of these benefits to his customers and asked them if this was something they wanted to add. "Given all of these benefits, is this something you want to add?" Unfortunately, he kept hearing, "No, thank you." Not only was he missing out on sales and commissions, but his customers were missing out on the opportunity to have their move go so much smoother. He realized that there were real consequences when his customers chose not to take advantage of these services. He's even had customers in the past become very upset when something they packed themselves had been damaged.

Justin decided to share some of these stories with his customers, and instead of asking them if they wanted to add these services, he would highly recommend them. "Taking advantage of these services will save you time and ensure your property against damages. In addition, you'll be all set up at your new place in no time. I highly recommend taking advantage of this. With your permission, I'll add it to your order."

This approach worked better, and it brought his sales up to the average for the company, but Justin still thought he was missing something. It turns out, Justin is still missing two vital elements for the correct formation of a "Recommendation Statement." First, he's not combining logical **R**easons, **R**ecommendations, and emotional **R**ewards. Justin is just making a value statement, followed by a **R**ecommendation. Second, he's not using **R**esearch to get the customer to recognize the **R**easons explicitly. The solution? Justin should conduct **R**esearch. Asking questions will help determine if the **R**easons to **R**ecommend this service actually exist for this customer. By asking the questions, the customer will explicitly state the **R**easons, making them so much more powerful when Justin uses them as evidence and support for his **R**ecommendation. Let's have a look at what this might look like:

"Have you set aside some time on the other end for unpacking and getting settled in?"

"Not really, the kids will be starting school, and we're going right back to work."

"Sounds like it's going to be busy, do you have a lot of experience with moves?"

"No, this is only our second move in the last 14 years."

"Since this is only your second move in a while and you're going to be super busy when you get to your new home, I'd suggest taking advantage of our packing and unpacking services. Having us do it for you will allow you to focus on settling in with your family and meeting your new neighbors rather than spending your nights after work unpacking boxes.

> Besides, you won't have to worry about anything getting damaged as our professional team will pack it and insure it just in case. With your authorization…"

When we ask questions allowing our customers to explore their own **R**easons, it validates our **R**ecommendation. The added information provided in our customer's responses enables us to add emotional **R**ewards for following our advice. To explain this strategy, I put the **R**esearch questions directly before the **R**ecommendation. In practice, these questions might have been asked much earlier in the conversation. In other words, you may ask your **R**esearch questions much farther in advance of your **R**ecommendation.

In Justin's case, he was looking for **R**easons to justify a **R**ecommendation he was planning to make. You will mirror this technique with the things you recommend all the time. Examples of this are extended warranties, certified installation, and specific insurances. In addition, you should always recommend yourself, your products and services and your company. There are several other ways to direct our **R**esearch to make a **R**ecommendation. We ask questions that will:

- Lead to a specific **R**ecommendation (Why me, why now, why my company, etc.)
- Determine whether we make a **R**ecommendation (Yes or No.)
- Determine which **R**ecommendation we will make. (A, or B, or more.)
- Validate our intended **R**ecommendation. (A only, regardless of response.)

In some cases, our customer's response to our questions will indicate which **R**ecommendation we make. Given two possible recommendations, A and B, I would need to ask questions and discover which would be most appropriate. Once determined, I can move forward with a "Recommendation Statement." An excellent example of this would be a professional recruiter trying to determine the best way to put a candidate's resume together:

"Are you most interested in continuing your role as a sales trainer, or are you more interested in remaining in the oil and gas industry?"

"Well, I'm more passionate about mentoring and training than I am about the specific industry, but my entire career has been oil and gas."

"That's not a problem, since your role is more important to you than the industry. Let's use language on your resume focused on your training skills and mentoring experience. This way, we can go after training roles in many different industries, and you can follow your passion."

In other cases, we may ask a question where any response leads to the same **R**ecommendation. As an example, one of my clients has an excellent value proposition. Due to the quality and reputation of their products, there are two major benefits to choosing their products for your home. First, their products have been shown to last longer than their competition. Second, installing their product in your home has been proven to increase the resale value of the home much more than their competitor's products. Here are two example dialogues:

"How long are you planning to stay in this home?"

"Just until the girls go off to college, two or three more years."

"In that case, I'd recommend Brand X as it's been proven to increase your home's value more than any other brand. When you sell the home in a few years, you can be confident you will maximize the sales price."

Or:

"How long are you planning to stay in this home?"

"At least 15 years, I'm pretty sure this is our "forever home."

"In that case, I'd recommend Brand X as it's been shown to last almost twice as long as any of the competitive brands. For the small added costs now, you won't have to worry about replacing it in a few years. Why buy two, when you can get one that will last twice as long?"

As you can see, the question, "How long are you planning to stay in this home?" really only has two responses. Long or short. If the answer is long, we can recommend this brand due to its longevity. If the response is short, we can recommend this brand due to its impact on resale value. Either way, the moment we ask the question, we provide ourselves with the ability to deliver a strong "Recommendation Statement" for this brand.

Summary

There are hundreds of different ways to deliver a "Recommendation Statement," and you should become comfortable with quite a few of them. Always consider your intended **Recommendations** in order to influence your **Research** questions. Allow your customer's responses to direct you forward. Don't assume the **Reasons** for your **Recommendations** exist. *Your advice will always have a much greater impact if you state the reasons the customer gave you, rather than those you may have assumed.*

What about those times when the best solution for your customer is not to recommend your products or services? That's easy. If you have no alternatives to offer, it's perfectly acceptable to say, "I don't believe this is the right product" or "I'm not the right person for the job." If you were a family law attorney and a friend came to you with a personal injury case, would you take it? I hope not. The same applies to any sales situation. If your products or services are not applicable, do the right thing, maintain your integrity, and give your customer the right advice.

Key Takeaways – Chapter 12

- You move forward through the sales process with "Recommendation Statements."
- **Recommendations** are strongest when you combine **Reasons** explicitly stated by your customer with **Rewards** connected to their priorities.
- Embrace flexibility and vary your language each time you make a **Recommendation**.

CHAPTER THIRTEEN
R6: THE VALUE OF RELATIONSHIPS

"The relationship isn't something you begin building after the transaction is over. Everything you've done from the moment of first contact, has set the stage for a future relationship to blossom."

THE VALUE OF RELATIONSHIPS

I introduced R6, **R**elationship, in Chapter Three where I explained that a **R**elationship is earned over time. While establishing a connection makes you human, building and maintaining a **R**elationship has greater long-term value. For some sales professionals, it is not always easy to put the value of a long-term **R**elationship over the immediate income from a single transaction. In my opinion, it is imperative that you do so.

Establishing a **R**elationship is becoming more and more essential to consultative sales. When a consumer finds a person who they trust and rely on, they will hold on for dear life. When they realize that you are on their side, they will go out of their way to continue to do business with you and refer others to you.

__The relationship isn't something you begin building after the transaction is over. Everything you've done from the moment of first contact, has set the stage for a future relationship to blossom.__ If you don't prioritize their well-being during the sale, you won't have a foundation for a relationship after the sale.

In most industries, there are five main benefits of establishing a longer-term **R**elationship with your customers. A positive **R**elationship increases customer loyalty, encourages customer advocacy, creates career sustainability, produces a more forgiving customer, and increases our intrinsic sense of fulfillment. Stated more plainly, you will have more repeat customers, more referral customers, a steadier income, more forgiving customers, and a more enjoyable career. Let's walk through each of these:

Customer Loyalty

In past engagements, I've often asked my audience to consider the value of one loyal client throughout a professional's career. When we add it all up, it can be quite significant. I've often heard lifetime values in thousands, hundreds of thousands, and occasionally in the millions. When we compare this with the value of a single transaction, the enormous advantage of fostering loyalty becomes quite apparent. Would it surprise you to know that repeat customers have a higher closing percentage and a higher profit per unit? It's a statistical fact. Repeat customers are less likely to negotiate the price and more likely to say, "yes."

For the purposes of this book, I'll focus on individual loyalty (as opposed to brand loyalty or organizational loyalty). Personal loyalty happens when a customer feels a sense of possession, as in, "my accountant, my lawyer, my insurance rep." Unfortunately, our clients remain our clients for only so long as they desire. They have the power in this relationship. If the customer doesn't take possession of you, you haven't earned their loyalty. In many different environments, I've heard the words, "Why is my customer working with _____?" or, "Hey, that's my customer!" If your customer doesn't remember you, isn't asking for you, and isn't reaching out to you, they are not your customer anymore.

Assuming you are good at what you do, the key to customer loyalty is generosity. When your customer genuinely understands that you care about them, and they believe in your ability and expertise, there is a social obligation for them to reciprocate and remain loyal to you. When I analyze the behavior of many sales organizations, I find that the only time they ever reach out to their customers is when there is money to be made. In essence, the only time the customer ever hears from them is when they are trying to sell something, which is the opposite of generous. When a customer identifies this behavior, it gives them all the social permission they need to spread their business around, rather than remain loyal.

My recommendation to you is to reach out to your customers when there is nothing in it for you. Ask them how their product or service is doing. Make sure all is well. Ask, "Is there anything I can do to help? Do you have any unanswered questions?" Whatever you do, don't combine, "I care about you," with, "I want to sell you something." Make sure you separate these touchpoints. Recently, I received a call from a company asking me how the product I'd purchased from them was doing. I replied that it was excellent. They immediately asked if I would take the time to go online and write a positive review. My recommendation to them would be to do this separately and space these two calls by 10 days or so. It would leave a much better impression at the end of the first call if they didn't ask me for a favor. I went from, "Wow, they really care about me and want me to have a good experience with their product," to, "Oh, they only called because they are trying to get positive online reviews."

Customer Advocacy

When a loyal customer becomes your advocate and promotes you to other people, they become your best marketing asset. Their endorsement goes a long way to beginning a transaction and relationship with another individual. When I analyzed closing percentages and profit margins, can you guess which opportunities were second place, just behind repeat customers? Yep, referral customers.

For a customer to refer someone to us, they have to trust us. They must have faith we will do an excellent job for the person whom they are referring. They are taking on a small portion of responsibility for the outcome when they recommend us and, therefore, there is an inherent level of risk for them. Our task then is to reduce that risk. There are many reasons for customers to recommend you, but the best of them is that they want to help both you and the customer they are referring. Your **R**elationship with them will help them take the risk. Remember to PREACH Luxury with your past customers as well as your present customers.

Career Sustainability

The most consistently successful sales professionals I've ever worked with all have something in common. They understand the tremendous value of building a network of loyal customers. In addition to providing a steady stream of opportunities, these customers are less likely to negotiate, more prepared, more enjoyable, and much easier to help. When we start a new career in sales, we have no network to draw from; we must "hit the pavement," and prospect for each and every opportunity. Ask anyone who's put in the time to build their network, and they will tell you, "It's a grind." Many would-be sales professionals decide to pursue other careers due to the difficulty of getting through this initial effort.

If we are lucky enough to work for a company that provides leads to work with, we still have to earn our way, and the number of leads provided may cap our potential. Only by supplementing these opportunities with loyal returning customers and their referrals are we able to push the limits and achieve at higher levels. When new opportunities slow down due to external causes, your network of loyal customers will keep you going. In a 10-year sales career with the same organization, how much of your business will be "new customers" in year one? How many will be repeat and referral customers in year 10? It's different for everyone, and it's entirely up to you. You have to earn it.

Intrinsic Fulfillment

When you compare a successful salesperson who has an established book of business with someone who does not, you will see an astounding difference in their every-day work life. While one is spending their time trying to win business from new contacts, the other is having personal conversations with folks they've known for a while. They are "catching up" with each other's lives, and the business end of things is simply something that's getting done while they are enjoying each other's company. It is a more enjoyable career. One is complaining that it's "slow," and the other is too busy to worry about it. They may both be exhausted at the end of the day, but one is frustrated, while the other is satisfied and proud.

Some have told me this is all wishful thinking. While I will concede that not all customers want to have a long-term **R**elationship, and this is impacted directly by the products and services we are responsible for selling, there are many successful sales professionals out there who have put in the time and realized the benefits of earning and maintaining a loyal following of customers. If you're not one of them, you may want to reconsider your long-term approach.

Creating a Forgiving Customer

In many industries, especially those that are service-based, there is another huge benefit to building and maintaining a positive **R**elationship with your customers. Positive **R**elationships are hugely beneficial for businesses that have a regular or semi-regular cadence of customer events. This includes, for example, hair stylists, accountants, attorneys, automotive service advisors, dentists, and many other roles. In any sales model where we have an ongoing business relationship, there is a high chance that at some point in time, something will go wrong.

If we've put effort into creating and maintaining a positive **R**elationship, our customers will be much more forgiving when something goes wrong. Ask anyone in these types of businesses if they'd like to have more forgiving customers. I am reasonably confident I know what they'll say.

BUILDING RELATIONSHIPS

During the typical customer lifecycle, there are three main opportunities to build a relationship; during the transaction, soon after the transaction, and longer-term. Your ability to establish a relationship with your customers at these moments will be crucial to sustainable success.

During the Transaction

My recommendations for you during the transaction should come as no surprise. PREACH Luxury and READ your customer. Be human, be yourself, and look for opportunities to relate to your customers and elevate their experience. Focus on solving the problem and satisfying the desire. As they realize that you are a caring person who has chosen to be on their side, they will feel lucky to be working with you. Thank them for working with you and find a way to personalize their experience. This is the beginning of the **R**elationship.

Soon After the Transaction

This is the phase directly after they have taken possession of the product, or the service has either just begun or just been completed. If it's an ongoing service, you will reach out after the first steps are finalized. If it's a completed service, you will reach out after it's done. If it's a product, you will reach out after the customer has acquired it, or it has been delivered and installed. This is your chance to show you care by following up with your customer, to make sure your solution met their needs and was not damaged or otherwise compromised. During this phase, you are verifying that they are happy.

Most importantly, this contact point must be all about your customer and have no explicit or direct benefit to you. This is not the time to ask for a referral or a positive review. Don't try to sell an accessory, additional services, or an extended warranty.

The moment the customer's phone rings, and they identify a salesperson on the other end, they absolutely believe you are about to ask them for something. You will surprise them in a positive way when you don't.

> *"Hi Mrs. Barron, it's Sophie with ABC. I just called to be sure everything was installed to your liking, and you are happy with everything."*
>
> *"Oh, hi, Sophie. Yes, everything is all set. We love it."*
>
> *"That's fantastic! I'm so happy it worked out so well. Listen, if you ever need any help with anything, even if it's just a question, please just give*

me a call. I'm here for you."

"Thanks, Sophie, you've been wonderful."

"Thanks, Mrs. Baron, you have a great evening."

Mrs. Baron is now staring at her phone, thinking, "Wow, she didn't even try to sell me anything. She really just called to make sure I was happy."

Over the Longer-term

Relationship-based contact is your greatest opportunity to remain memorable, and it is your best chance to create long-term loyalty and advocacy. What would Mrs. Baron think and feel if Sophie called six months later, just to see if there were any unanswered questions and to be sure everything was still working correctly? What if Sophie called two years later, just before the warranty expired to make sure there weren't any outstanding issues? Do you want to stand out as a true sales professional? This is how you do it.

I've had the pleasure of working with some excellent sales professionals over the years, but this particular experience is worth sharing. I worked with an automotive salesperson who made the type of calls described above. One afternoon, he received a call from his customer:

"Hey Tim, it's Jonathan Williams."

"Hi Jonathan, what can I do for you?"

"Well, you know how you always say if I ever need anything, I should call you?"

"Of course."

"Well, it's my wife's birthday, and I'm throwing a surprise party. Today's been crazy, and traffic is horrible. I don't have time to get the cake and get home. The bakery is right next door to your dealership."

You know what happened next, right? Yes! Tim picked up the cake and delivered it to the surprise party. To this day, he has a framed photo of him, the husband, the wife, and the cake, along with a handwritten letter from Mr. Williams. It's displayed proudly in his office as proof of how much he cares about his customers.

All sales professionals should be so lucky as to have an opportunity like this. Without the effort Tim put in to creating and maintaining a Relationship, that call would never have happened. You've probably heard of the ABCs of selling, "Always Be Closing." I want you to replace this with, "Always Be Caring." Positive Relationships built on mutual loyalty, and sustainably successful careers in sales, go hand-in-hand.

MAINTAINING RELATIONSHIPS

Maintaining a positive Relationship with your customers doesn't need to be complicated. Your goals should be to remain memorable and valuable to your clients. Over the longer term, there may be opportunities to sell products and services. If you have put effort into the Relationship, these opportunities will be much easier to approach and much more rewarding.

My advice? Be memorable, be valuable, and don't sell until it's appropriate to do so. When you do recognize an opportunity, explore it with your customer through Research. There are many ways to stay in touch with your customers that add value and are non-aggressive. Here are some examples I've collected from folks I've worked with over the years. This list is anything but exhaustive, however I do hope it will spark some ideas:

- Write handwritten notes. These go a long way toward personalization and showing an extra effort. You're handwriting's bad? Print nicely. At our last home, we had our front door repainted. Afterward, we received a handwritten card from the painter saying, "Thank you so much for allowing me to add to the beauty of your home." Very simple. Very memorable.
- Send postcards to all of your customers on a semi-regular basis. Some of the variations I've seen in different industries include, "The quote of the month," or "The recipe of the month." These are

examples of providing something for your customers and asking nothing in return. Sure, some of them get thrown away, but many of them end up magnetized to the refrigerator - with your name on it. Feel free to modernize this through email or social media.

- Create and send out a personal newsletter (snail mail or email) once a year. The several I've seen have different elements but always have a big "thank you" to all clients. Sometimes these are paired with local charities and fundraisers. These are usually sent out just before the holiday season.
- Reach out with a random phone call, text, or email just to check-in and make sure everything is good. Communication like this is best with products that have a long life-cycle like appliances, computers, and automobiles.
- Use social media as a way to stay professionally connected to your expanding group of customers and advocates. There are many excellent resources available to learn about this and understand how others are using it.

What are the opportunities to show your customers you care about them during their life of ownership? How will you sustain and maintain a positive **R**elationship without basing it on a transaction? What can you do for them, that is not also for you?

Key Takeaways – Chapter 13

- A positive **R**elationship with your customers will provide a steadier income and lead to a more enjoyable career.
- **R**elationships begin with unselfishness. Show your customers you care about them.
- Over time, loyal customers are more valuable than new customers (but only if you earn it).

CHAPTER FOURTEEN
R7: FOCUSING ON RESULTS

"Only if you are willing to give external factors credit for your success, can you blame external factors for your failure."

ACHIEVING RESULTS

The last "R" in The Seven Rs of Selling is **Results**.

When I discussed this in Chapter Four, I encouraged you to first form your own internal definition of success. Your initial goal doesn't have to be sales-related. Perhaps your goal is to earn enough extra income for a vacation. Or maybe you'll define success based on the total number of positive online reviews you receive from your customers. On the other hand, maybe you just want to be recognized as the best. Whatever it is, there are three main ways to break down your daily habits and behaviors to begin measuring **R**esults and improvement:

Quality, Quantity, and Community

These factors refer to the effectiveness of your effort, the volume of your effort, and your ability to work well with others in your organization. I'm sure you've heard the phrase, "It takes a village…" Well, quality, quantity, and village just didn't sound right to me. On a more serious note, let's take a look at each of these.

Quality

Quality refers to the strategies, behaviors, and tactics you employ as you perform each task. I've dedicated this entire book to improving the quality and effectiveness of your interactions with customers. I'm hoping that, by this point in the book, you've decided to try a few of the ideas I've shared in previous chapters. While I won't attempt to summarize everything under this one heading, I will share my thoughts on how to go back and incorporate these ideas into your everyday sales practice. My best piece of advice is, "Don't try to do it all at once."

Imagine taking a golf swing and having your partner say, "Your feet are too far apart, and your standing too close to the ball. Your grip is too tight and too open. You need to stand more upright and keep your eye on the ball. Don't forget to keep your left arm straight and flatten out your wrist at the top of the backswing. You've got to start the downswing with your lower body and make a full shoulder turn. It's all about shifting your weight as you rotate. Make sure you release through the ball and follow through. You're not relaxing and letting the club do the work." I don't know about you, but if my golf buddy said this to me I might let him see my club "up close."

All of the strategies and techniques in this book are a bit like that. R7, STEP, PREACH, READ, LIVE, and NAVIGATE: a nonstop avalanche of advice. There is virtually no way to incorporate everything all at once, so begin with the fundamentals. At the very core of *The Sales Upgrade* is the idea that selling is about helping. You are an advisor, guide, and consultant. Your job is to provide advice. Work your way through The *Seven Rs of Selling* with a focus on your **R**ecommendations. If you are delivering strong "Recommendation Statements," it means a lot of other things are coming together.

Choose one or two things you would like to incorporate and practice them consistently. Organize a list of things you would like to master, and prioritize them. As you develop new skills, move on to the next item on your list. Successful selling is as much, or more, about the process as it is about skill and ability. Diligent process execution is more critical than "raw talent." You will be incorporating what you do with how you do it: both mechanics and behaviors.

If you consider the elite athletes of the world, you will realize that they are achieving amazing things not only due to raw physical ability but due to diligence, practice, dedication, hard work, and perseverance. In many cases, the only reason that they have raw physical ability is that they've worked so hard to develop it. When these athletes are "in the arena," they give it everything they have. They don't look back and say, "I could have tried harder." I personally learned this lesson when I was about 12 years old. I was on a swim team. In one particular relay race, I was the fourth man up. By the time it was my turn to dive in, we were in last place out of six teams. Demoralized, I dove in and swam my laps. To my surprise, we came in second place, about three yards behind the winner. While my teammates cheered, I felt a crushing regret. I had more to give and I knew it. We could have gone from last to first. I've wanted to go back in time and swim that race again my whole life. It was a valuable lesson.

Quantity

I've spent a lot of time in many different sales environments, and I've seen the daily routines or lack thereof of thousands of sales professionals. We've all heard the phrase "work smarter, not harder." Here's another popular saying, "If you want something done, ask a busy person to do it." My suggestion? Work hard *and* smart. As you improve the quality of what you do, maximize your effort through organization, prioritization, and time management. Take a fresh look at the way you do things with an eye toward efficiency. If you are a "two finger typist," it might be time to learn how to touch type. This alone might double your efficiency. There are plenty of courses available at minimal cost.

Organize your efforts to spend the majority of your time on sales-related activities. This means prospecting for, and communicating with, potential customers, rather than surfing the web or catching up with others at work. Balance your time and effort between achieving both short-term, and long-term, success. It's too easy to focus on winning new customers at the expense of your long-term **R**elationships. Manage your time based on the size and impact of your opportunities. Instead of selling toothbrushes and cotton swabs to the dental offices you are calling on, advise them on how they could expand their practice and cut out the middleman by purchasing their own machine to make crowns on-site. Upgrade their dental chairs and recommend a new autoclave. Spend time doing the cost-benefit analysis with them.

Community

In sales, we need our support system: sales management, peers, receptionists and greeters, fulfillment and order processing, delivery, installation, and customer service. The better we work with everyone else around us, the better the customer's experience will be. This enhances the value of the product or service you represent as well as your chances for a viable long-term customer **R**elationship. Your ability to collaborate as a team member could make the difference between, "Oh, you worked with Nick on this? He's fantastic," and, "Oh, you worked with Nick on this? Let me go through the paperwork again and make sure he didn't mess it up."

Don't be a prima donna. Yes, you are selling more than everyone else. Congratulations. You are taking advantage of the environment and the circumstances around you, and you are working hard and smart. Well done! Success is not a good reason to believe the culture and rules surrounding your organization do not apply to you. Being a top performer is not a good reason to isolate yourself from others. There isn't usually a good reason to complain about management or all the meetings you have to attend. Don't abandon professionalism and common courtesy. If you do, at some point in the future, your employer may decide that the negative effect of your toxicity outweighs the benefits you bring to the company. If this is you, and your workplace was a game of Survivor, your colleagues would vote you off the island.

SELF-AWARENESS

The adage used to be "leave your personal stuff at home." I think most of us can agree, that's not really an option. I believe that the best course of action is to be aware of what you are "carrying around" with you from day-to-day. You know yourself better than anyone else. If you are aware of your state of mind, you are capable of choosing what you want to share with your coworkers and customers.

Do a mental check when you're interacting with other human beings and make the choice to show up in the right frame of mind. Always remember, an essential element of what your customers are paying for is a positive experience. With all the choices available today, we can't afford to drop this particular ball. The good news? Showing up for someone else and elevating their experience also elevates our own.

Discomfort = Growth

Your awareness of self will also be an advantage as you begin to practice *The Seven Rs of Selling*. We are rarely good at new skills the very first time we try them. If you are replacing old sales habits with new ones, you may experience a slight decline before you become proficient with new skills and techniques. This is another reason not to try all of these new ideas at one time.

Before you realize the upside, you will need to put in the work to develop the skill. As you try new things, they may feel uncomfortable at first. This discomfort is also known as personal growth. Every time you get past that awkward feeling, you've grown. You are now more well-rounded and adaptable to more situations. As your skills improve, your results will follow.

Someone I respect once told me that the most powerful person in the room isn't the one who's most dominant, it's the one who's most versatile and adaptable. Don't use, "That's just not my style," as an excuse. Practice it, get good at it and it will become one of the styles you have available in your repertoire.

Don't Blame the Hammer

Having worked with salespeople, and having been a sales professional for most of my adult life, one thing is almost always guaranteed. When we don't succeed, we always have a reason. We blame the CRM system, the competition, the paperwork, the pricing, the incentives, the pay structure, the product, the process, the internet, the customer, and the boss. The list is endless, and I've heard most of them.

When you are tempted to blame someone, or something, other than yourself, take a look around. Is anyone in the organization successfully navigating these same circumstances? If so, the issue isn't external. The most consistently successful sales professionals have learned to blame themselves, which allows them to focus on their internal behaviors and improve. When a carpenter doesn't hit the nail on the head, they don't blame the hammer. When we, as sales professionals don't "nail it," we shouldn't either. When you accept responsibility for your success, you open yourself up to adaptation and growth. ***Only if you are willing to give external factors credit for your success, can you blame external factors for your failure.*** Before you give all the credit away, consider this question: If external factors are responsible for your success, why do we need you?

Eat the Frog

Mark Twain once said, "If it's your job to eat a frog, it's best to do it first thing in the morning. And if it's your job to eat two frogs, it's best to eat the biggest one first." The moment you start to dread something is the moment you should do it. Get it over with. Whatever it is, it isn't going to go away. Left alone, that frog will get bigger, hairier, and wartier; and it will insert its ugly little head into everything else you do. It will increase your stress, absorb your mental and emotional energy, and deplete your ability to bring everything you can to your human interactions. When you don't eat the frog, it doesn't hop away.

Once you've eaten the frog, however, you've accomplished the most challenging thing you'll have to do today. It's all downhill from here. You will feel relieved, even happy. And this is what you'll be bringing to all of your human interactions. When eating the frog becomes a habit, you will gain the reputation of someone who does not shy away from the difficult tasks. As you begin tackling the tough stuff first, you will soon learn that many of the things that seem like frogs turn out to be chocolate instead.

Hit the Reset Button

Sometimes, in spite of your efforts, you will find yourself in a difficult place. Maybe a customer treated you poorly, or a big sale fell through. Perhaps something has occurred outside of work to put you in the wrong frame of mind. The worst thing you can do is to take your frustration, anger, or disappointment into your next conversation. When you are self-aware enough to see and feel this happening, I encourage you to "hit the reset button." This is a quick and easy exercise I've been teaching (and using) for years.

To do this, you need to create your personal reset button. Here's what I want you to do. Ask yourself this question, "What five words would you want every one of your customers to use when describing you?" If you're anything like most people, words like; professional, kind, knowledgeable, fun, honest, and helpful are springing to mind. Once you have your own five words, take the time to create a one-page document with only these five words on it. Make sure the font is something you like, and the size of the text is as big as possible while keeping all five words on a single page. Now print it out and put it in your desk drawer. Read it once every time you start your shift and put it back in your drawer. You've just created your personal reset button. Use it when necessary.

Self-evaluation

As you strive for greater and more significant results, your ability to self-evaluate will be critical. As R7 is an "in the moment" strategy, the best time for an internal evaluation is directly after any customer interaction. This could be a face-to-face meeting, phone conversation, or an email exchange. Ask yourself these questions:

- Am I connecting and relating to my customers?
- Am I elevating their experience?
- Am I taking control of the process and acting as an advisor?
- Am I asking the right questions in the right way?

- Am I moving through the process with "Recommendation Statements?"
- Am I interacting and engaging when presenting my products and services?
- Am I handling price issues with more fluidity?

Your answers will provide you with a quick self-evaluation. Over time, you will be able to STEP through your process, PREACH luxury, READ your customer, LIVE your product, and NAVIGATE price with greater proficiency.

Key Takeaways – Chapter 14

- Focus on delivering strong "Recommendation Statements," and the rest will fall into place.
- Manage your time and maximize your efficiency.
- Don't be a prima donna. Leverage your support system.
- Take responsibility for your own success.

PART FOUR:

TAKING ACTION AND MOVING FORWARD

CHAPTER FIFTEEN
APPLYING R7

"When you are dealing with someone who has already asked a question or expressed interest, stop marketing and advertising! You should be advising, guiding, and communicating."

OUTBOUND INITIATIVES

In this chapter, I want to help you apply the concepts laid out in this book to all the different ways that you communicate with your customers. There is a massive difference between a customer who has "raised their hand," and a customer who has not invited you to contact them. Even customers who have volunteered for some form of contact can often display hesitancy at the start of sales conversations. For this reason, I encourage you to read through the first section on "Outbound Initiatives," even if you don't usually do any "cold calling" or outbound unsolicited prospecting. It will only make you stronger when dealing with an uncommitted customer.

In the written communication section, I'll discuss best practices when dealing with a prospective customer over email, who has either asked for information or provided their contact information to you as an interested party. In the final section of this chapter, we'll discuss inbound phone calls from customers, and how to identify opportunities and move them forward in the sales process.

The Sales Upgrade applies differently to outbound lead generation. When a customer reaches out to us and effectively says, "I'm interested," it is much easier to assume the role of an advisor, guide and consultant. If we receive an email or a phone call from a customer seeking answers or requesting information, it's our job to help them. Entering the conversation in this manner allows us to don the mantle of an advisor more readily.

Conversely, if we are reaching out to a prospective customer who has not requested contact with us, we must convince them we *can* help them. All of your outbound activities under these circumstances are closer to marketing than they are to selling. Dealing with a "hand raiser" is much different from reaching out to someone who hasn't raised their hand at all.

This chapter is not meant to be a comprehensive guide to marketing, outbound prospecting, cold calling, lead generation, or business development. There are other resources available for those specific skills. In this chapter, I want to provide some advice on how to use the methodologies in this book when reaching out "cold" in different scenarios.

The entire goal of outbound lead generation is to get our prospective customer to say, "Yes, I could use help with that," or "Yes, I would like to hear more." In essence, we are trying to convert them from an "involuntary prospect" to a "voluntary opportunity." The moment this transition occurs, you can use R7 and the other models as I've laid them out. Since many, "involuntary prospects" can be a bit skittish, I recommend taking a more delicate approach to the use of R7 and the other strategies. That way, you won't have to deal with the rejection of scaring off a potential customer. (Did you see the "Recommendation Statement" in those last two sentences? I'm practicing what I'm preaching).

Let's walk through the models presented in *The Sales Upgrade* as they apply to outbound prospecting:

The Seven Rs of Selling

Research

With an "involuntary prospect," you will not be able to do as much real-time **R**esearch as you would if they reached out to you. Peppering them with questions is going to encourage them to run for the hills. However, before you contact your prospect, you can (and should) do as much **R**esearch as is reasonably possible, given the size of the opportunity. The amount of **R**esearch you do should be commensurate with the value of the opportunity. You are asking them to invest time (and potentially money) with you. They should understand that you've invested a bit of your time in them. If you are selling $20 raffle tickets to raise money for the local charity, your **R**esearch will be minimal (and potentially non-existent). If you are selling a time-share for a multi-million dollar yacht, you will want to do quite a bit of **R**esearch before you reach out.

Depending on your product, service, and industry, you will be referencing different data points. Websites and social media should provide you with quite a bit of information to begin with. With this information in hand, do a bit more **R**esearch to find something that might be of interest to your prospect. You could provide them with an article, study, white paper, or testimonial. This little piece of value might be the key to opening the door to a conversation. Regardless of the amount of **R**esearch you do, you will want to have at least one compelling question prepared. This applies to all forms of correspondence.

If your product or service is more detailed or complex, you may want to begin with an open-ended question to spark a more involved conversation and gain an understanding of your prospect's situation. A closed question could shut your conversation down prematurely and negate the work and effort you put into your **Research**. If your product or service is more basic, you may want to formulate a compelling closed question. This will create efficiency. In the raffle ticket example above, your question might be something like, "Would you be willing to support breast cancer research with a small donation of only $20? You'll also be entered in a raffle to win …?" Because it's a small-ticket item (quite literally), and you haven't invested any time or effort, you can afford to lead in with a "yes" or "no" question and deal with a higher rate of rejection. If they say, "no," you learn and move on.

Rapport

Timing can be critical when it comes to building **R**apport with an involuntary prospect. You may only get the chance to ask one question, so prioritize grabbing their attention and converting them to a voluntary opportunity. Use your question to spark interest in your offering, rather than something that will lead to **R**apport. You can still reveal something personal, but don't overdo it. Make sure it relates to something the customer has voluntarily shared. Once the customer expresses interest, and opens up to a deeper conversation, you can then lead the conversation toward your "Strategic Reveal" if it's still necessary.

Reason – Recommendation – Reward

If the start of your conversation goes well, it's logical to assume that you will have a "call to action" at some point in your conversation. What is the logical next step for them to take? Use a "Recommendation Statement" to move them in the right direction. Remember, they did not initiate the conversation or come to you for advice or help. They did not ask for help. Once they do express interest in moving on to the next step, keep your Recommendation soft. How would you respond to unsolicited advice? Lead in with, "Here's what I'd like to suggest as next steps," rather than, "This is what I recommend you do."

Relationship

Though you might not believe that the **R**elationship is a key factor with unsolicited prospecting, your approach could have a profound impact over time. Your ability to keep things professional and handle rejection with grace will set you up for potential future success while also giving you the ability to work with pride, rather than frustration.

Take a long-term approach and assume you will have a conversation with this same prospect in the future. How would you like them to remember you? Even if you meet with rejection, thank them for their time. Remember, they didn't ask you to interrupt their day! "Thank you for your time. I know that even two minutes isn't easy to give, and I really do appreciate it. Have a great rest of your day." Watch your tone, maintain your integrity, and display professionalism.

Results

Outbound prospecting is a daunting task that can also be quite rewarding. Someone beginning a sales career will find this especially true. As you measure your results, quantity and quality will make a huge impact. Get good at it. Do a lot of it. Measure your success ratio, as well as your volume of activity.

Take a brief moment after every contact and ask yourself what you could have done differently. Analyze the different pieces of your approach. What is your initial introduction? What questions are you asking? What is your call to action? How are you positioning yourself personally? Develop your talents and put in the effort. Over time, you will achieve excellence.

STEP, PREACH, READ, LIVE, and NAVIGATE

Each of these applies to unsolicited prospecting. STEP will help you frame your goals during each phase of your conversation. Pay special attention to recommending only the very next step in the process, rather than trying to move too far too fast. PREACH will help you elevate their experience. READ will keep you grounded "in the moment" as you correspond or converse. As you communicate with them, keep the READ program running in the background and be hyperaware of any opportunities to relate, elevate, or advise. LIVE will be your tool to pique their interest in your offering and predispose them toward your call to action. Use a question to engage them in the problem, and then show them how your solution solves it. NAVIGATE will inevitably come in handy as they consider the economics of your proposal.

Additional Advice

- If you have an email address and a phone number, email first and call second. It's easier to lead in with, "I'm calling to follow up on my email," than it is to say, "Hi, my name is xxx, and you've never heard from me before."
- If you are using email as your prospecting tool, don't send the same email twice. Change the language every time. Three emails with different language = persistence; three of the same emails = spam.
- Reference social proof. Telling someone you can help them is never as effective as someone you've already helped telling their story.

EMAIL CORRESPONDENCE

As discussed at the very beginning of the last section, there is a vast difference between someone who has not requested (and is not expecting) contact from you, and someone who is. When you are trying to get someone to express interest and become a voluntary opportunity, you are marketing and advertising. ***When you are dealing with someone who has already asked a question or expressed interest, stop marketing and advertising! You should be advising, guiding, and communicating.***

Many of the organizations I've worked with in the past have combined or confused these approaches. Go back and take a look at your emails. Are you advising and guiding an individual who has expressed interest, or are you advertising and marketing to someone to create interest? I would advise you not to do both in the same email. Choose one or the other, based on the immediate goal you are attempting to accomplish.

For this section, I will assume you are dealing with a prospective customer who has expressed interest in your products or services in some way. Effectively, they have "raised their hand." Whether this customer has reached out directly to you via email; requested information via your website or another online source; or provided information to a third party, lead provider, they have essentially said, "I want information," or, "I want help."

Email Appearance

The first thing I would suggest is viewing your email from the perspective of your customer. They have reached out to you in some way for information or guidance. What are you sending them in return? Below are a few guidelines based on my experience with successful sales organizations and professionals:

- Make sure your emails read well on a smart phone or tablet. Currently, studies show that people open about two-thirds of their emails on mobile devices, and this has been increasing every year. If you are B2B, this may be a bit lower, depending on your industry. If you are B2C, this is probably higher. As it turns out, black text on a white background is pretty effective. "Text only" emails will size the text to the default setting of the individual's phone. If you are going to include graphics in your email, narrow graphics are better than wide graphics. Phones will re-size the email to fit the screen; the wider the graphic, the more everything will "shrink" to accommodate, including your text. If your customer has to "pinch out to zoom," or do a lot of scrolling to read your email, you should consider changing the format.
- Keep it short. In general, the longer it is, the less likely it will be read. Consider your goals. If your email is getting too long, you may be trying to do too much in one email.
- Don't make it look like spam. It's not an advertisement. Try to avoid producing an email with colors, too much emphasized text, large fonts, or emojis and other symbols.
- DON'T USE ALL CAPS! STOP YELLING AT YOUR CUSTOMER.

- Use proper grammar and punctuation, but don't get too wordy. Read your email out loud, does it sound like something you would say?
- Be realistic with your subject line. Reference your customer's question or request, so they know what it is. "The answer to your question regarding ABC Accounting Services," is way better than, "Your Fabulous New Accountant!!"
- Be human with your greeting and your signature. In the United States, "Dear" is a very uncommon personal greeting (and usually means what you are about to read is a template). Instead, use, "Good morning, good afternoon, or good evening." As in all things, use your judgment based on your culture, your industry, and your personal preferences.

Email Content

The content of your email should be extremely strategic. Above all, remember that you are a consultant, advisor, and guide, and your email should convey this tone. You are not a salesperson, and you are not a customer service person. You are here to help them with your knowledge and expertise. Below is the framework I typically suggest. Unlike previous lists, I put this one in order as I suggest you do it chronologically:

1. Answer the customer's questions. Earlier in this book, I've indicated that customers don't always know the best questions to ask. It's the same with emails but, unlike real-time conversation, it's more challenging to help your customers understand this. If you are receiving a request for information, it's safe to assume your competitors are also receiving a request from this customer. If you don't answer their question and your competitor does, the rest of your strategy won't matter because your customer will drop you like a hot rock. By not answering their question, you have disqualified yourself. However, when you do answer their questions, be sure to use the strategies in this book to move the conversation forward.
2. Introduce the complexity of your product or service offerings. Give them more information than they've requested. Often our

customers have a simple question, such as, "How much is it? Is it currently in stock?" or, "Are you licensed and insured." By introducing complexity, you increase the need for your expertise. "How much do you charge for a manicure?" might be met with, "We have basic and premium nail services starting from $30. There are more than 15 different choices available, depending on the statement you want to make with your nails."

3. Ask a question to engage them in dialogue. The most significant challenge with electronic lead sources is initial engagement. A simple question encourages a response, which leads to more involved dialogue. Ask more specific questions than you might in person. For example, a kitchen designer might say, "Tell me about your project?" but in an email might ask, "Will this be new construction or a remodel?" which is much easier for the customer to answer. Make sure your question is strategic. It should be something that makes them curious or provides you with an opportunity to relate and elevate.

4. Provide a clear call to action in the form of a "Recommendation Statement." What is the very next step the customer should take to solve their problem or satisfy their desire? Why should they take this step? What will they get out of it emotionally? If you've successfully introduced complexity, maybe the next step is a phone call to discuss their situation and simplify things. A smaller step will be easier for them to agree to and will move the process forward. Whatever you do, don't end your email with a "let me know" statement (you promised).

5. Give yourself permission for future follow up. If you intend to send another email in the future should this customer not respond, tell them that you will be reaching out again. "I want to be sure I answer all your questions and provide the most help I can, so if we're unable to connect today, I'll try again tomorrow (or next week, etc.). This makes it perfectly acceptable to maintain your follow up cycle (assuming you're follow up cycle doesn't include five more emails in the next 48 hours).

 **1 ANSWER THE CUSTOMER'S QUESTIONS**

 **2 INTRODUCE COMPLEXITY**

 **3 ASK A STRATEGIC QUESTION**

 **4 PROVIDE A CALL TO ACTION**

 **5 CREATE PERMISSION TO FOLLOW UP**

Additional Advice

- If you use templates, take the time to customize the response to each customer. A cut-and-paste email isn't premium. PREACH Luxury and take the time to fine-tune your response.
- Don't use nested questions in an email format. If you ask several questions in the same email, you've just made it difficult for your customers to respond. Instead, use your call to action to move them to a phone call or face-to-face meeting. Asking multiple questions in an email is a clear indication that you are trying to move too far, too fast.
- READ your customer when you are responding by email. Be hyperaware of opportunities to relate to them on a human level and elevate their experience. If you look for them, you will find them. This could be a question they've asked or even in the email address they're using. If their email address is hugesteelersfan@

xyz.com, this is an opportunity. Don't miss it. If they asked about "the red one" they saw in your showroom, go take a picture of it (possibly with you in it), and send it to them with your reply.

INBOUND PHONE INQUIRIES

The R7 methodology, and all of the accompanying models, can be applied to incoming phone calls from customers. This section will give you additional insight into these specific situations. Below are the most common pitfalls I have observed, as well as my advice.

Be Proactive, Not Reactive

Your prospective customer calls in, and you pick up the phone. They begin with a question, and you answer it. They ask another question, and you answer. Congratulations, you are basically an information kiosk. By a wide margin, this is the most common reason for failure on the phone. It is a global epidemic. It's like an old-school black and white horror movie. Cue the screams, "Oh, no! I've got information kiosk!" As a consultant, advisor, and guide, you must lead the conversation. To be proactive, you must move to **R**esearch as quickly as possible. You become the leader once you begin asking questions. If your customer asks a good question, feel free to answer it and then ask your own question. If they ask a poor question, diffuse their question by introducing complexity, and then move to your next question.

As an example, if they ask, "Can you tell me what differentiates you from your competitors?" feel free to answer, as that's an excellent question. If they ask, "What do you charge by the hour," you might say, "Hourly costs vary based on the depth and complexity of services you need. Can you tell me a little about what you are hoping to accomplish?" This strategy would also be better for your customers because the price is only a good comparison when the value is fully understood. If you charge $80 per hour and someone else charges $40, are they still less expensive if they take three times as long, or do the task half as well? In my experience, most of the questions our customers ask are limited in nature and lead to weak competitive comparisons. Help your customers understand this by being proactive.

Go Micro, Not Macro

For you to be proactive, you must have goals and a process in mind before you even pick up the phone. When there's an opportunity on the other end, what should happen at the end of the call? This is your macro step. Now you have to determine all of the micro-steps that you will need to accomplish before you make your final **R**ecommendation (more on this in the next and final chapter).

If you are a student of R7, you will want to relate on a human level and build trust, as well as find **R**easons and **R**ewards for your intended **R**ecommendation. Imagine calling a wedding planner and asking, "Are you available for June 20th?" and having them respond with, "Yes, I am available. When can we meet so we can begin planning your special day?" I don't know about you, but I might have a few more questions before I agree to a meeting. This wedding planner should take control with **R**esearch. Something like, "What aspect of your wedding would you like to be most memorable?" This would allow the conversation to open toward relating, elevating, and establishing more value. Focus on the next step, not the final step.

Ask Good Questions

You will lead the conversation with questions. I devoted an entire chapter to the art of asking good questions (Chapter Ten), so I will not go into too much detail here. When you are on the phone with your customer, you should ask questions that do one of the following:

- Provide you with the ability to relate to them on a human level.
- Open up possibilities for you to elevate their experience.
- Engage your customer in a two-way, meaningful product/service presentation.
- Help you fully understand their situation so you can provide appropriate advice.

Every question you ask should be valuable to your customer. Many organizations want to track the success of different forms of advertising, so they ask, "How did you hear about us?" This question provides no value to your customer. If you need to ask this question, I recommend asking it at the end of the sale, rather than the beginning of a phone call. What you really want to know is, "Does this advertising source create sales?" not, "Does this advertising source generate phone calls?" Use your questions strategically. Don't use "yes" or "no" questions if you don't want to hear "no." Don't force a decision until you are quite confident your customer will make the right one.

Get Contact Information Early

Regardless of your skills and the excellence of your products and services, you will inevitably run into some customers who do not accept your call to action on the first phone call. You may want to have the ability and permission to follow up with them. To achieve this, you will need your customers to provide their contact information voluntarily. I believe you should do this as early as possible. If your process allows, and it makes sense for the customer as well, do this before your primary call to action. This will avoid awkward situations like this:

"I'd suggest we meet in person. Would later this week work for you?"

"Well, I'm just not ready for that. Let me think about it."

"OK, in that case, can I have your phone number?"

Ha! Good luck with that approach. If you've already answered their questions, they may believe they don't need you anymore. With this in mind, they feel they don't need to provide contact information. A useful technique is to make the collection of information about them instead of you. "I have a pdf brochure as well as technical specs on that product, what email address should I send that to?" or, "I will keep you abreast of any changes in pricing or programs that come out regarding that, is your mobile the best number to reach you?" It's an excellent strategy to get their email address or phone number first and then ask for their name. Psychologically, once they've given you a phone number or email address, they understand they will have to provide you with a name to go with it. Avoid the temptation to simply capture their caller ID and use that for follow-up. It may, or may not be the right number to reach them, and even if it is, they didn't give you permission to use it.

I typically advise asking for their last name first. This avoids getting their first name and then having them say, "Just call me Frank," when you ask for their last name. Ask with, "How do you spell your last name?" instead of, "what's your last name." This is an "autoresponse" and bypasses their decision process. They will simply spell their name. I've also observed that most people will pronounce it before they spell it. This avoids having to ask two questions instead of just the one.

Avoid the Product Dump

LIVE Your Product! In Chapter Eight, I introduced you to this method of providing engaging presentations of your product or service. This concept is just as important on the phone as it is in person. When we are face-to-face, we have our customer's reactions to guide us, and the ability to interact with the product or service as an avenue toward engagement. This isn't the case on the phone, so be careful that you don't fall into the trap of thinking that your customer is completely enthralled with your five-minute detailed monologue about how great your stuff is. I have bad news; they've been checking their watch and rolling their eyes for the past four and a half minutes.

If you find yourself talking without a customer reaction for more than 30 seconds, ask a question and engage them in the conversation. In many cases, their curiosity about your products and services is a great **R**eason to **R**ecommend moving to the next step in your process.

By All Means, READ Your Customer

A phone call is a real-time experience with your customer, and all of the strategies in this book apply. Don't miss the opportunity to shine. After every phone call, ask yourself, "What do they know about me?" If the answer is nothing, you are missing a golden opportunity to differentiate yourself from your competitors and add value to your offering. Listen carefully for that opportunity to PREACH Luxury and elevate their experience. When the time is right, make a **R**ecommendation based on both logic and emotion. I've witnessed too many sales professionals, who are absolutely amazing in person, turn into an information kiosk on the phone.

1. BE PROACTIVE, NOT REACTIVE
2. GO MICRO, NOT MACRO
3. ASK GOOD QUESTIONS
4. GAIN CONTACT INFO EARLY
5. AVOID THE PRODUCT DUMP
6. READ YOUR CUSTOMERS

Key Takeaways – Chapter 15

- The strategies in *The Sales Upgrade* must be used delicately until your customer expresses interest.
- R7, STEP, PREACH, READ, LIVE, and NAVIGATE may be applied to all communication formats once a customer "raises their hand."
- Don't be an information kiosk. Lead the conversation by asking strategic questions.

CHAPTER SIXTEEN
CUSTOMIZING YOUR SALES UPGRADE

"If there is a reason for it, you should be recommending it. If there isn't a reason for it, why do you offer it?"

BUILDING YOUR OWN RESOURCES

Once you've decided to move forward with *The Sales Upgrade*, you will need to adapt these ideas to your sales environment. While I've provided quite a few examples from many different industries, only you can hone these strategies for your unique situation. In Chapter 14, when discussing Results, I introduced some key concepts that should get you started. In this chapter, I will ask you to break things down on a practical basis so you can adjust *The Sales Upgrade* strategies for everyday use. Let's look at each of the models I've introduced to you:

BUILD YOUR OWN RESOURCES – THE SEVEN Rs OF SELLING (R7)

To fully use *The Seven Rs of Selling*, you will first need to consider all of the possible **Recommendations** you might make throughout your sales process. Take the time to brainstorm this. Chances are, there are quite a few possible **Recommendations**. Start with your sales process and break down all of your macro and micro-steps. You will move through your sales process with a variety of **Recommendations**, (more on this in the very next section). Now move on to your brand, product, and service offerings.

Do you work with a particular brand or multiple brands? If one brand only, make a list of your brand's key differentiating factors. If you work with numerous brands, make a list of each brand you represent.

There are consequences to not moving forward with your products and services. Every product or service you offer should have a **Recommendation** to go with it. Start by making a list of the most popular product and service **Recommendations** you might make. Finally, move on to options, accessories, add-ons, and alternatives. Every potential choice should have a **Recommendation**. Think about it; why do you have this alternative, that option, or any particular accessory? *If there is a reason for it, you should be recommending it. If there isn't a reason for it, why do you offer it?*

At this point, you should have:

- A list of process step **R**ecommendations
- A list of brand **R**ecommendations
- A list of product and service **R**ecommendations
- A list of accessory, option, add-on, and alternative **R**ecommendations

The next step will be to begin brainstorming **R**easons for every **R**ecommendation. Consider your brand list. What are the reasons for the customer to move forward with any given brand? Does this brand solve problems that other brands don't? Is this brand more desirable than other brands? If so, why? Make a list of all the **R**easons to **R**ecommend any given brand you represent.

What are all the possible **R**easons to move forward with the next process step? What are all the **R**easons to **R**ecommend any one particular product or service over another? What are the **R**easons to move forward with any specific option, alternative, add-on, or accessory? You now have **R**easons to go with every **R**ecommendation on your list.

It's now time to consider the emotional **R**ewards of following these **R**ecommendations. What does the customer stand to gain by following a particular **R**ecommendation? What will they stand to lose if they don't? How will you phrase these in more emotional language? Based on each of your **R**ecommendations, come up with a list of emotional **R**ewards. Relief, pride, joy, safety, confidence, and contentment are all **R**ewards for moving forward. The reduction, or elimination, of pain, stress, worry, and doubt are all **R**ewards for following your **R**ecommendations. Now you have **R**ewards to go with all of your **R**easons and **R**ecommendations.

Now that you have the resources for your **R**ecommendations more clearly defined, you can begin constructing your **R**esearch questions. What questions will you ask to discover whether or not these **R**easons exist for any particular customer? You will want these to be plainly stated by the customer. If the **R**eason can be assumed, find a way to ask your question anyway. As an example, we can assume that reliability is an essential factor when choosing a parachute. If reliability is one of the strong **R**easons to recommend a particular parachute, we might ask, "What are the three most important qualities you're looking for in a parachute?" I would hope that some form of, "I'm looking for one that opens every time I pull the cord," will make the list. **R**easons stated by the customer are much more meaningful and persuasive than **R**easons assumed by the sales professional.

Now you've created an invaluable toolbox of **R**esearch questions. For the consultative phase of your sales process, the only, "R," you're missing is **R**apport. Consider the lessons learned in Chapter 11, "Intentional Rapport." What is your "Strategic Reveal?" In the context of your sales process and considering your mix of products and services, what question can you ask to lead to your reveal?

Using your "Strategic Reveal" intentionally will allow you to learn something about your customers and connect your truth to theirs.

Everything is now in place for a consultative sales process. Customized for your environment as well as your personal reality, you have what you need for **R**esearch, **R**apport, **R**easons, **R**ecommendations, and **R**ewards. You are officially armed and dangerous.

From here, you can move on to the **R**elationship. What are the non-sales follow-up steps you can add to your repertoire over time? Review Chapter 13; what can you do in the short- and long-term to prove that you care about your customers and not just their money? Put these on your calendar every time you finalize a transaction and be ready to complete these tasks: tailor your messaging, consider what voicemail you will leave, and purchase thank you cards, so you have them on hand.

Dedicate time in your day to maintain **R**elationships with past customers. Whatever you choose to do here, don't let "I don't have what I need, I don't know what to write, I don't have time, I don't know what to say," or, "I forgot to put it on my calendar," be your excuse.

Lastly, track and measure your **R**esults. Break your process down, so you know what needs to improve. Focus on one area at a time and refine your materials, your approach, and your behaviors. Let each failure be a tool for future improvement. Remember: quality, quantity, and community. Are you doing things correctly? Are you doing them enough? Are you a harmonious part of the team, or a royal pain in the behind?

Don't blame the hammer, do eat the frog and when you really need to, hit the reset button. Remember that discomfort = growth. You are responsible for your own success. Take ownership and be intentional. Whatever you do, please do it in service to your customers and take pride in what you are contributing.

BUILD YOUR OWN RESOURCES — STEP FORWARD

Building a set of resources to enable you to smoothly and intentionally transition between the steps in your sales process is not all that daunting. To practice "Outcome Orientation," you must lead the process and be intentional at each stage. You should begin by mapping out all of the most significant (or macro) steps in your process. Next, fill in the micro-steps that need to be taken before moving on to the next macro step.

As an example, if you've just completed a face-to-face meeting and the next big step is signing a written contract, consider all of the small things that have to happen before you can make that **R**ecommendation. Perhaps your written proposal will need to be customized? While you are working on that, you may have to have an additional phone conversation with your customer to clarify the details. Will your proposal need to be reviewed or approved by anyone in your organization before you present it to your customers? Once completed, you will need to send the proposal to them, and you may want to confirm receipt. The customer may wish to have a conversation to answer questions and clarify details before signing. Will there be another meeting? Should there be another meeting? Do you want to present your solution in person, over the phone, or electronically?

As you consider all of these details, make a list of everything you should attempt via a "Recommendation Statement." The phone call to clarify details, the phone call to review the proposal, and the potential meeting to sit down and sign the contract would all be possible **R**ecommendations. As you walk through your process in this manner, make a list of every macro and micro-step that could or should be recommended. Use the techniques in the prior section on *The Seven Rs of Selling* to establish the **R**easons and **R**ewards for these **R**ecommendations, and then formulate your **R**esearch questions.

If you've taken the steps above, you will know what's next for your customers at any given moment. Furthermore, you know all the small things that have to happen to get there. Lastly, you are prepared to move through the process using **Recommendations**, and you've established the logical **Reasons** to do so, as well as the emotional motivation for your customer. This is the **Strategic** part of STEP.

As you begin moving through your process more intentionally, you will realize there is a flow to it. Follow the plan. If you've mapped out your steps appropriately, the completion of the micro-steps signals the need to move to the next macro step. It's crucial to learn to recognize this moment. If you haven't completed the in-between stages and you are trying to move to the next big step, you will come across as aggressive, your customer may not be ready, and you risk failure. Moving too soon to the next macro-step without completing the micro-steps is, by far, one of the most common mistakes made by salespeople. If you are a design and build firm, don't sell the complete remodel in the first meeting. Sell the design! You don't get to do the job if they don't buy the design. If you are an attorney that does estate planning, don't sell your overall plan, sell the face-to-face meeting. Focus on selling step by step. The full package will follow and you'll be ready to knock it out of the park.

Conversely, if you don't move forward when the opportunity presents itself, you risk over communicating, and you may create discomfort and indecision. Too much information and unnecessary conversations are awkward. Once you've mapped out your process, this gets easier. Keep a mental checklist (or a physical one), and when the checklist is complete, use a "Recommendation Statement" to move forward in the process. This is the **Timely** part of STEP.

Now that you are more in control of what is happening with your customer, as well as what *will* be happening, you can explain future steps to your customer proactively. Put yourself in your customer's shoes, review your process step by step and ask yourself, "What should the customer know before it happens? What should I proactively explain?" Build the explanation of the process into your sales process! Imagine this statement from the salesperson using the example above:

"I've really enjoyed meeting with you both and spending time with you. Now that I understand your situation more clearly, I can put a custom proposal together to move forward. I'll be working on that over the next couple of days. To be sure I've captured all the details, may I give you a call with any clarifying questions? Wonderful. Once my proposal has been reviewed and approved internally, we can set up another meeting to go over it and move forward. I want this to be convenient for you, so I can easily come to you. I don't want you to stress or worry about the time it takes to come all the way here. Which day would work best for you later this week?"

By explaining your process to your customer and allowing them to see what moving forward looks like, you are intentionally creating a scenario where it is much more likely to happen. The more vividly you paint the picture, the more likely it will come true. As each step progresses, it will confirm your expertise, rather than act as another hurdle the customer has to jump over. By explaining the process and next steps so transparently, you demystify what is happening behind the scenes, and your customer becomes much more comfortable. This is the **Explicit** part of STEP.

Lastly, consider the customer's experience as you spend time with them. It's not sufficient to go through the steps mechanically. How do you want your customers to *feel?* What do you want them to experience? What would you like them to say when they describe their sales experience with you and your organization? With this in mind, pay special attention to how you execute the process, rather than just the execution of the process itself. This is the **Purposeful** part of STEP.

BUILD YOUR OWN RESOURCES — PREACH LUXURY

Preparing yourself or your organization to PREACH Luxury is mainly a mindset. Do you see your customer's experience as an extension of your products and services? Do you recognize how it can create value and differentiate you and your brand? If your answer to these questions is "Yes," there are definitely some things you can do within your organization to improve your customers' experience.

Proactive

Take a critical look at your organization, your sales process, and your individual customer situations. How can you improve everyone's experience by doing things in advance, providing more than is expected, and explaining things before you are asked to do so? Make a list of these things and incorporate them when possible. Continue to grow this list with every customer you work with.

Real

Honestly, there isn't much you can prepare for here. For those of you who have a genuine nature and a concern for your customer's wellbeing, this will be easy. For some of you, I suggest redefining what success means for you. Is it sales at all costs or customers first?

Easy

This is where a lot of opportunities exist to prepare in advance. Walk through your sales process and look for opportunities to simplify the experience for your customers. Prepare everything you can in advance, and coordinate your efforts with others inside and outside your organization. Search out ways to reduce any waiting time for your customer. Be relentless in your pursuit of making things easy for them.

Accommodating

Look for ways to personalize and tailor the experience for customers in your environment with "Situational Tailoring." What does your organization already do to enhance your customer's experience? Take a look at each of these and find ways to personalize and tailor each of them. In some cases, it will be how you do it; in others, it will be what you say when you do it.

Consistent

Look for ways to brand your customer's experience. Find something that you can do for every customer, every time. Choreograph your customer's visit before they arrive so everyone involved can add value to the experience. This will provide consistency between the people who work with your customers. Be true to your organization's promises to customers. Follow through and do what you say you will do. Be consistent with your own promises. Celebrate your successes and help spread your practices to others in the organization.

Human

You've prepared all your life for this. Be yourself. Be genuine. Be amazing! What makes humans different from other species is our ability to consciously choose how we show up every day. What will you bring to the world today? What will be your contribution? You have the power to make this choice. Use it!

BUILD YOUR OWN RESOURCES – READ YOUR CUSTOMER

The best way for you to prepare to READ Your Customer is to practice. You will develop and fine-tune this skill as you experience everyday situations. Listen for those opportunities to relate and elevate in all customer service and sales conversations, even when you are the customer. Listen for these opportunities when you hear the conversations of your colleagues.

Most importantly listen for these opportunities in your own conversations. When consequences are involved, are you asking your customer what they want to do, or if they want to do it? Or are you giving advice?

Mentally review your conversations directly after you have them. Did you miss any opportunities to relate or elevate? Did you provide advice at the right time in the right way? This is your chance to self-correct. Keep a log of missed opportunities. Every time you add to that list, it's a lesson learned, and you've given yourself a better chance of seeing that opportunity the next time around.

If the opportunity to relate, elevate, or advise isn't present, are you intentionally moving the conversation forward by asking a question? Is there an uncomfortable pause? Did you start reacting to the customer instead of leading the discussion? Develop your skills in forming and asking questions. If things don't go the direction you intended, it may be due to a poorly formed question or the lack of any question at all. This latter situation usually ends up with the customer taking control by asking a question. Think back to the questions you asked in each of your conversations. Are there opportunities to refine your questions?

Once you develop this skill set, you will see an immediate improvement in your connection with your customers, your control over the conversation, and your closing ratio. When you create trust, elevate the customer's experience, and provide meaningful advice, it will be so much easier for your customer to follow your lead.

BUILD YOUR OWN RESOURCES — LIVE YOUR PRODUCT

Interactive and engaging product and service presentations require some preparation on your part. First of all, you need to know your products and services inside out. Put the time in, do your homework, and stay up to date with new products, alternatives, features, options, and accessories. If your business is service-based, stay up to date with the changes in your industry and your practice.

Analyze your presentations in real-time. Are you doing all the talking? Are you covering the products, options, alternatives, features, and benefits that are priorities for this customer or merely telling them what you like about it? Are you just telling them everything you know? Stop yourself from giving a one-way product dump. Engage your customers.

Here are a few ways to prepare yourself. Make a list of three to five main priorities your customers might have when considering your products or services. As an example, for a surround sound system, the main priorities might be feature set, sound quality, ease of installation, immediate availability, and price. In your conversations with customers, use your questions to discover which priorities are most important to them. What's their main priority? What doesn't matter to them at all? Here's an example:

"So, what are you looking forward to most in a surround sound system?"

"Are you kidding? The Superbowl's in two weeks! I can't wait."

"Got it, are you considering professional installation?"

"No, I was hoping to install it myself."

After listening to this customer's responses, what would you say are this customer's priorities? I would say:

1. Immediate availability
2. Ease of Installation
3. Sound quality
4. Feature set
5. Price

It's totally fine if your list is different, but I do hope ease of installation, and immediate availability made your top three. With this particular customer, I might end up recommending a wireless system, so no wires will have to be run through walls. Because I listened well, I will **Verify** that the system I recommend meets this customer's needs by describing the ease of installation. I will be sure to inform my customer that it is immediately available and in stock, and as I describe the sound quality, I will be sure to highlight any features related to live sports. I probably will not go in-depth on the feature set and, as of now, price isn't even in the equation. Even if the price is attractive, or a discount is being offered on this model, I probably won't mention it (yet).

If you make a list of customer priorities for your main products and services and use your discovery skills to mentally prioritize these features, you will be in a great position to excel at the **Listen** and **Verify** sections of LIVE Your Product. To know your customer's priorities, you will need to ask the right questions and listen well. As you move to your presentation, tailor the features and benefits around this customer's preferences.

Think about how your customers could engage their senses and **Interact** with the product during your presentation. Is there something to touch, see, smell, taste, or hear? In the above example, we can easily use touch, see, and hear:

"This model even has a stadium mode where you can hear the fans surrounding you. Let me show you how easy it is. See the mode dial? Just turn that two clicks clockwise. Perfect, can you hear how the sound quality changed? Now it sounds like we're sitting in the arena."

If you are service-based, use point-of-sales materials, diagrams, video testimonials, or other physical materials. As you move through your presentation, ask and direct your customers through the available interactions. Too many salespeople I've come across do all of the interactions themselves, "Here, let me change it to the stadium mode… sounds good, right?" Any time you are tempted to interact with your product in front of your customer, ask yourself if the presentation would be more meaningful if the customer did it instead. If so, you know what to do.

Your customer is interacting with the product, and you are highlighting the features and benefits that are priorities for this specific customer. The last and final step is to **Engage** them in the presentation and make it a two-way conversation. In Chapter Eight, you learned that we do this by asking specific questions. Your questions will serve two purposes here. First, you will be having a two-way conversation. Second, the question you ask will be explicitly engineered to highlight the importance of this particular feature for this specific customer. Continuing to use the sound system example, here are some examples:

- "It sounds like you'll be connecting the system to your main television, how important will voice clarity be for you?" (Feature highlight - voice clarity).
- "Will this system be for one room in your home, or are you looking for a multi-room or whole-home system?" (Feature highlight - multi-room, wireless capability and expandability).
- "What are all of the devices you'll be connecting to the receiver?" (Feature highlight - connectivity, multiple inputs, ease of use).

To best prepare for these types of presentations, make a list of the product's significant features and benefits that you want to highlight, and then brainstorm the questions you could ask to lead to your feature presentation. The questions you ask are specifically designed to bring the importance of a particular feature to your customer's attention. By moving through your presentation in this way, you will involve your customer in a two-way, engaging, and interactive presentation. Interaction, verification, and engagement all add value to your offering. Besides, the customer is enjoying the process of being educated and informed.

BUILD YOUR OWN RESOURCES – NAVIGATE PRICE

Preparing to NAVIGATE Price in your unique environment requires you to take a hard look at your organization; your products and services; your facility and location; your process; and yourself. Step into your customer's shoes and consider all of these factors through their eyes. In Chapter Nine, I introduced the idea that price is always connected to value. To best prepare to handle price issues with customers, you will need to discover all possible ways to create value.

Begin by looking at your brand as a whole compared to others. Are there advantages to working with your company compared to your competitors? How are you positioned? What is the brand image? What does your organization have, do, or provide that others don't? Brainstorm with your colleagues and create an exhaustive list of the aspects of your organization that create value. Make a list of everything you can think of. Some examples include:

- Family owned and operated
- In business for more than _____ years
- Heavily involved in the community
- Employee-owned
- On the _____ list of the best companies to work for
- On the _____ list of the fastest-growing companies

Begin weaving these into your conversations with your customers. Ask questions that allow you to divulge these value-adding factors:

"Are you familiar with our organization?"

"Have you worked with us before?"

"Do you know anything about our company history?"

Next, consider the positive aspects of your products and services. Are they higher quality, more aesthetically pleasing, more durable, or longer-lasting? Do they have more options, features, or accessories than your competitor's products and services? Is there a better warranty? From a service perspective, do you offer more experience, more flexibility, more options, or alternatives? Again, think of everything you possibly can and make a list. As you LIVE Your Product, include and highlight these factors, especially if you discover that any of them are priorities for your customer.

Move on to your process. Maybe your products are virtually the same as your competitor, but your method is better, more streamlined, more enjoyable, or simply more valuable. Try to see your process as a customer would.

Recently, I worked with a BMW dealership to help them integrate a video-based, multi-point inspection into their service process. As the technicians complete the physical inspection, they take videos of the critical areas of the vehicle. Each customer receives a narrated video of their vehicle. They can see the condition of their tires, brakes, and suspension, as well as the engine compartment and underside of the car. They can see their fluids have been topped off, as well as the measurement of their tire tread depth and the thickness of their brake pads. Anything being recommended is now visible to the customer. They can see if there's a missing bolt, oil leak, belt-tension issue, or other needed repair. This process provides a high level of transparency and trust.

The short-term value is the immediate sale of service work because the **R**easons for the **R**ecommendations are plainly visible to the customer, and there is a higher degree of trust. The long-term value is in customer satisfaction, future loyalty, and customer retention. As customers learn to value this addition to the process, they won't want to service their vehicle somewhere that doesn't have this added service. This process will become part of this organization's brand value. Importantly, in this case, neither the product or service has changed. This dealership isn't repairing or maintaining vehicles any differently than before; nor are the parts any different than you would get at another certified BMW service center. It's only the process and experience that's changed.

You should also take a look at your facility and location. Are you more conveniently located? Do you have a nicer facility or environment for your customers? Do you have more locations than your competitors? As before, make a list of everything that could be considered a competitive advantage, such as larger inventories, faster time to production, or immediate availability.

Finally, consider everything you bring to the table. Are you able to READ Your Customer and PREACH Luxury? If so, you are adding enormous value to the products or services you're selling. What are you doing for your customers that others don't? Have you connected to your customers on a human level where others haven't? Have you elevated their experience when others did not? You are your own brand, and your personal brand has value.

At this point, you should have a list of competitive advantages and differentiating factors for your organization; your products, and services; your locations and facilities; your process, and yourself. Review them all and choose the most impactful and essential from among them. Design your **R**esearch by constructing a set of questions engineered specifically to introduce these advantages and value-adding factors.

All of this is engineered to boost value. As value increases, price sensitivity decreases. When the price does become a pivotal point in your conversation, use the rules in Chapter Nine to overcome objections and NAVIGATE Price. Practice! Every time price becomes an issue, use it as a learning experience. What could you have added to the conversation earlier to increase the value? Did you pause when you delivered the price? Are you focused on selling your products or solving the customer's problem? Are you validating the price or apologizing for it? Did you treat a question about the price as if it were an objection? Are you imposing your own value system on your customers? Are you advocating for your customers when a discount is needed to close the sale? Do you need to take something away to fit the customer's budget? Are you approaching every sale with passion, enthusiasm, and energy?

Don't blame price for your failure. Ask yourself constantly why your products and services are priced the way they are; your customers will surely want to know. The more prepared you are to proactively answer these questions before your customer asks, the less price will be a problem.

BUILD YOUR OWN RESOURCES – BRINGING IT ALL TOGETHER

Reading through this chapter should have kickstarted your efforts to customize *The Sales Upgrade* to your style and your environment. As you organize your materials and create your playbook, focus on the basics, and build on them. Each day, add a little more to the resources you've created. Begin organizing them into a personal toolbox. You've "downloaded" *The Sales Upgrade*, but you still have to execute it. As you become more proficient with R7 and each of the accompanying models, I am confident you will see real results.

Key Takeaways – Chapter 16

- Build your resources. Applying these models to your specific organization and situation will bring R7 to life in your environment.

- The more you upgrade your sales strategies, the more value you create for your customer, your organization, and yourself.

- If you began reading The Sales Upgrade as a salesperson, I hope you'll finish as a consultant.

CHAPTER SEVENTEEN
FINAL THOUGHTS

"You are the most essential part of the value chain. You are the differentiating factor, and you are the key to an enjoyable customer experience."

THANK YOU!

Thank you for taking the time to read *The Sales Upgrade*. Writing this book has been an enriching experience for me. I genuinely hope it has been a rewarding experience for you, as well. I am not a professional author. *The Sales Upgrade* is the very first book I've written and could quite possibly be the only book I'll ever write. I didn't write this book in a cabin in the woods, at a cozy desk, in a quiet place. I wrote it in airplanes, hotel rooms, and other in-between spaces as I traveled to and from various sales environments. My day job is working with sales organizations and sales professionals just like you.

So, thank you for your involvement and your commitment to the world of sales. Those of you who pursue a career in sales in service to your customers, with an ethical and moral imperative, are the unheralded champions of the coming evolution. The insights and models I've written in this book are the patterns and behaviors I've seen practiced by successful sales professionals all over the world. These are the talents and skills I've observed from you, and so many others like you. Observing and learning from people like you, discovering successful patterns and behaviors, and organizing these habits, skills, and techniques into a sharable format has been my life's work.

I absolutely love what I do, and I have a passion for helping people realize their potential. As I stated in the introduction, you don't have to agree with, or adopt, all of the ideas presented here, but I sincerely hope you found value within the pages of *The Sales Upgrade*. If you increase your performance with even one of these ideas, I will be proud of the time and effort I've put into these pages.

You are the most essential part of the value chain. You are the differentiating factor, and you are the key to an enjoyable customer experience. However, as good as you are, there are always opportunities to improve. Helping people advance from below average to acceptable performance is rewarding; helping people grow from acceptable to above average is exciting; being the catalyst to help sales professionals transition from above average to truly and consistently exceptional is life-changing and exhilarating. For me personally, this is the pinnacle of achievement.

Thank you for your willingness to embrace new ideas. As you begin working with your very next customer, STEP Forward, PREACH Luxury, READ Your Customer, LIVE Your Product, NAVIGATE Price, and take the first steps toward mastering *The Seven Rs of Selling*.

WHAT'S NEXT?

Let's Connect

Stay in touch with me and gain access to additional information and resources:

Visit My Website

Go to **www.hansjvanorder.com** to learn more about me, access my blog, view additional resources, and see what else I'm up to.

Join The Sales Upgrade Community

Sign up for my newsletter at **www.hansjvanorder.com/newsletter** to stay up to date with my thoughts and ideas and be the first to hear about workshops and events.

Speaking Engagements

To discuss content, messaging, and availability for speaking engagements, contact me directly at **hans@driveperformance.com**.

Business Performance Consulting, Coaching, and Training

Visit Drive Performance's website at **www.driveperformance.com** for more information on our services. Let's discover how we can improve your sales performance, elevate your customer experience, and develop your leadership team.

Host a Workshop for your Organization

In addition to the workshops we host at our facility, we offer large and small-group workshops at our client locations. For more information, email **info@driveperformance.com**.

ACKNOWLEDGEMENTS:

There are many people to acknowledge and thank for their help while bringing *The Sales Upgrade* to life. First of all is my wife, Jennifer. This effort would not have been possible without her love, support, and encouragement. In addition, she has substantially and directly contributed to the content, ideas, and quality of this book. Thank you, Jenn. With a family our size and my travel schedule, you've still got it all together; and we are thriving. You are a rock star!

To all my colleagues at Drive Performance, who have helped me bring these methodologies to the real world, I owe a tremendous debt of gratitude. You are all consummate professionals. Thank you for your hard work and honest feedback. This book wouldn't be where it is without your help. With special thanks to Amanda Perkey, Christopher Duncan, and Justin Wingfield.

I would like to thank Andrew Dawson and Mary Hoekstra, my editors. Thank you for your editorial prowess as well as your excellent opinions, thoughts, and ideas for improvement. Your input was invaluable. A big thanks to Heather Wullenweber at Moonlight Creative for her wonderful work on the infographics, and Ashley Bugg at Little Nest Portraits, for making me look presentable in the author photo.

Lastly, while the models, concepts, and strategies presented in this book are uniquely my creations, it has been the thousands of successful sales professionals I have worked with through the years who have provided the root behaviors, practices, and tactics that underlie their fundamental structure. Thank you to all of you for sharing your genius, your hard work, your successes, and your failures.

ABOUT THE AUTHOR:

Before becoming an entrepreneur in 1999, Hans Van Order enjoyed a successful career in sales and sales management. From selling rodeo tickets via cold-calling, to leading a team as the director of a mortgage bank (and just about everything in between), Hans refined his sales approach in the everyday melee of genuine sales environments.

Hans is the CEO of Drive Performance, where he leads a team of consultants who train, coach and mentor successful individuals and organizations across multiple industries. He and his team have designed and facilitated sales, leadership and customer experience curriculums for BMW Group, Sub Zero and Wolf, and many other brands.

As a keynote speaker, Hans has captivated and motivated audiences at national sales conferences, corporate events and industry roundtables. His passionate, genuine and engaging way of presenting and articulating ideas inspires actionable results.

Hans has a bachelors' degree in business management from Pepperdine's Graziadio School of Business and Management and is working to complete a master of science in organization development.

Hans grew up in the bay area of San Francisco, spent 10 years in Orange County, CA, and fifteen years in Pittsburgh, PA (Go Steelers!). He's been known to enjoy a good bourbon (neat, one-cube, old fashioned…surprise me!), and as you no-doubt know by now, he's the father of four boys. Hans currently lives with his family in Charlotte, North Carolina.

* * *

www.ingramcontent.com/pod-product-compliance
Lightning Source LLC
Chambersburg PA
CBHW030320100526
44592CB00010B/502